WORDS TO LIVE BY

The Best of Indian Non-fiction for Children

Deepa Agarwal has written more than 50 books for children and adults. *The Wish-fulfilling Cow and Other Classic Indian Tales* (Scholastic India, 2015) and an anthology – *100 Great Poems for Children* – (Red Turtle, 2015) are two of her recent titles. Deepa has won the NCERT National Award for her picture book, *Ashok's New Friends* (Children's Book Trust) and her adventure novel, *Caravan to Tibet* (Penguin/Puffin, 2007) was selected for the IBBY Honour List 2008 as the best book from India. Five of her books have been listed in the White Raven Catalogue brought out by the IYL, Munich.

WORDS TO LIVE BY

The Best of Indian Non-fiction for Children

EDITED BY
DEEPA AGARWAL

hachette INDIA

First published in India 2016 by Hachette India
(Registered name: Hachette Book Publishing India Pvt Ltd)
An Hachette UK company
www.hachetteindia.com

SRD

ISBN 978-93-5009-945-2

Hachette Book Publishing India Pvt Ltd
4th & 5th Floors, Corporate Centre;
Plot No. 94, Sector 44; Gurgaon 122003, India

Typeset in ITC Korinna Std 10/14.5 by
by Manmohan Kumar, New Delhi

Printed and bound in India
by Manipal Technologies Limited, Manipal

Contents

Introduction

Is non-fiction simply writing that provides information? Some might think so. The pieces we have collected in this book, however, are far more than that. They are the real life experiences of real people who share the sources of their inspiration, the impassioned speeches and letters of women and men dedicated to causes, reminiscences – sad, comic and inspirational, fascinating glimpses into the lives of animals and reptiles as well as exciting travel tales. They are revelations from great achievers and leaders and nuggets of knowledge shared by experts in their fields.

Mahatma Gandhi's autobiography, *The Story of My Experiments with Truth*, is a book that I reached out for eagerly as a young girl. What impressed me was how frankly the Mahatma exposed his struggles. In the extract we have, Gandhi tells us about his school days, presenting a picture of a sensitive boy devoted to the truth, and shares the lasting impression mythical heroes left on him – permanent but hard to explain. He says, 'My common sense tells me today that Harishchandra could not have been a historical character. Still both Harishchandra and Shravana are living realities for me, and I am sure I should be moved as before if I were to read those plays again today.'

'My father, do not rest. Do not allow us to rest. Keep us to our pledge. Give us strength to fulfil our promise, your heirs, your descendants, your stewards, the guardians of your dreams, the fulfillers of India's destiny.' This is what the illustrious poet Sarojini Naidu said in her stirring speech on the radio when Gandhiji's assassination plunged the nation into mourning. Her words still resonate powerfully, reminding us that noble ideals do not die even though the person who embodied them may have departed this world. And who can deny that Gandhi's principles continue to inspire people throughout the world?

In the summer of 1928, ten-year-old Indira Gandhi was beating the heat in Mussoorie. Her father Jawaharlal Nehru was in the plains, plunged in the freedom movement. He kept the father-daughter relationship warmly alive through a series of letters, which also continued to educate in the most affectionate manner. These letters dealt with a variety of subjects – from the beginning of this earth to the development of civilization and government. Our extract from *Letters from a Father to His Daughter* is about the development of monarchy. Nehru talks frankly about the deterioration of this system: 'Kings forgot that they were really chosen by the people in order to organize and distribute the food and other things of the country among the people. They forgot that they were chosen because they were supposed to be the cleverest and the most experienced persons in the tribe or country. They imagined that they were the masters and all the other people in the country their servants. As a matter of fact, they were the servants of the country.'

Nehru taught Indira in this delightful manner. However, a friendly system of education for the young was in the minds of many iconic personalities. Rabindranath Tagore began his school Patha Bhavana, which later grew into the famous university of Santiniketan, because he believed that children should acquire learning in a free and natural environment, without the pain of excessive discipline, so they enjoy the process. In this extract from his work *Personality*, Tagore frees children from the tyranny of textbooks and exams, saying: 'At any rate during the early period of education children should come to their lesson of truths through natural processes directly through persons and things.' What a wonderful time the students must have had in his school!

Elders control children's lives, it is true. In 'Life at My Own Pace', a humorous yet poignant piece about his childhood, much adored writer Ruskin Bond talks about his love for walking which lets him enjoy nature from close – exactly what Tagore wanted for his students. And what possibilities Bond's Granny's orchard in Dehradun presented! He says, 'I made friends with an old jack-fruit tree, in whose trunk was a large hole in which I stored marbles, coins, catapults, and other treasures much as a crow stores the bright objects it picks during its peregrinations.' But in the end we encounter what Tagore wished to save children from – the insensitivity of the schoolmaster who thoughtlessly misplaced precious letters – from Bond's deceased father.

Ruskin talks about his deep bond with his father, and so does another inspiring figure from our times – Justice

Leila Seth. 'Memories of a Father and a Home' is an extract from *On Balance*, her moving and insightful autobiography. She remembers the treasured time when she got to know her father better during an illness that confined her to the house. He shared his beliefs and his love for books, which stood her in good stead because sometime before her twelfth birthday, sadly, he succumbed to an illness. 'So it was a very quiet and lonely birthday; truly the age of reason had arrived and it was a clear and cold dawn. There were no friends, no gifts, no warmth. But Aunty was wise; she presented me with Louisa May Alcott's *Little Women*, and I became totally absorbed in it.'

The chapter from former Indian president Dr A.P.J. Abdul Kalam's bestselling autobiography *Wings of Fire* is on a less personal note but also about growing up. It reveals how a dedicated teacher can inspire his students to reach for the skies, as Kalam literally did. He shares how he developed a lifelong interest in science and mathematics, and acquired the principles that made him such a respected figure of our times. 'Iyadurai Solomon, who later became a Reverend, taught me that before anything I wanted could happen, I had to desire it intensely and be absolutely certain it would happen. To take an example from my own life, I had been fascinated by the mysteries of the sky and the flight of birds from early childhood. I used to watch cranes and seagulls soar into flight and longed to fly. Simple, provincial boy though I was, I was convinced that one day I, too, would soar up into the skies. Indeed, I *was* the first child from Rameswaram to fly.'

Yes, the lives of great achievers do offer important lessons for living. In Sudha Murty's 'Aapro J.R.D.' we learn the importance of never giving up, whatever the odds.

After completing her postgraduate degree in engineering, Sudha noticed an advertisement from Telco, the famous Tata company, which stated 'Lady candidates need not apply'. Furious at this discrimination, she decided to apply and also wrote an angry postcard to J.R.D. Tata, pointing out that the Tatas had been pioneers in many fields but were being unfair to women. She was amazed to get an interview call and convinced them to give her the job. She gives all the credit to J.R.D., saying: 'I consider J.R.D., a great man because, in spite of being an extremely busy person, he valued one postcard written by a young girl, who was asking for justice and questioning him.'

The freedom movement was an inspiring time in our history and idealistic revolutionaries like Bhagat Singh valiantly battled the excesses of the colonial government, and even forfeited their lives for the cause. Bhagat Singh's sacrifice is well known, but not many of us are aware that he was an intellectual giant, an avid reader and an inspired writer. He wrote four books in jail, which were smuggled out and unfortunately got lost. Some of his speeches and other writing have survived. In his 'Statement before the Lahore High Court Bench', Bhagat Singh effectively demolishes the arguments of the sessions judge who awarded a life sentence to Batukeshwar Dutt and Bhagat Singh himself in the Assembly Bomb Case. In this powerful and moving statement, he points out that the judge never took their intentions into account. Using the example of Jesus Christ who was put to death because his ideals were not recognized by the rulers of that time and the opposite one of General Dyer who killed hundreds of innocents but was rewarded, he makes a strong case about what true justice actually may be. According to him, it means understanding the motive behind any action. He explains and vindicates his and his companion's actions in these eloquent words: 'Bombs and pistols do not make revolution. The sword of revolution is honed on the whetstone of ideas. This is what we wanted to emphasize.' In other words, when they threw the bombs, they did it to draw attention to the plight of their colonized countrymen and did it in such a manner that they did not inflict mortal injury upon anyone.

Subhas Chandra Bose, another shining light of the time, gave many stirring speeches. We have included his 'Address to the Women's Section of the Indian Independence League, Singapore' to provide an insight into a historic moment. The Azad Hind Fauj had been born, but Bose had more ambitious plans. In this address he acknowledges the contribution of Indian women to India's freedom movement. He asks them to continue nursing wounded soldiers, but wants more – that emulating the Rani of Jhansi, they take up arms against the enemy. And thus the famous Rani of Jhansi regiment of the INA was born. Bose said: 'To those who say that it will not be proper for our women to carry guns, my only request is that they look into the pages of our history. What brave deeds the Rani of Jhansi performed during the First War of Independence in 1857! Similarly, many brave women like the Rani of Jhansi are required in our Last War of Independence also. It is not important how many guns you can carry or how many cartridges you can fire. It is the spiritual force which will be generated by your heroic example that is important.'

Talking about spiritual force, who embodies it better than Swami Vivekananda? A young man from a well-to-do

Bengali family, he was drawn so strongly to spiritualism that he became a sanyasi, wandering the country. When Vivekananda attended the Parliament of the World's Religions in Chicago, USA, the closing words of his short speech which introduced the west to Hinduism, struck a deep chord: 'I am proud to belong to a religion which has taught the world both tolerance and universal acceptance. We believe not only in universal toleration, but we accept all religions as true.' He received a two-minute-long standing ovation from a crowd of seven thousand people!

There are other motivating pieces as well in this book. The brief biography of famous scientist C.V. Raman written by Dilip Salwi, a well-known writer of popular science and science fiction, outlines Raman's determined quest for knowledge and his extraordinary achievements. In another article for science buffs, the focus is on 'Indian Astronomy'. The great scientist and science writer Jayant Narlikar has explored the story of the development of scientific knowledge and astronomy in our country in his book *The Scientific Edge.* In this passage he focuses on the contribution of Raja Jai Singh of Jaipur in this field.

Knowledge, good education and social justice are explored in several other pieces. In his address delivered at the Convocation Ceremony of the Karnataka University, the great educator and former Indian president Dr Sarvepalli Radhakrishnan shows great concern that students understand what it means to be completely educated. For him it includes good values as well as scientific knowledge and in the following sentence he lays stress on the influence of good literature: 'Our generation in its rapid travel has not achieved the habit of reading the great books and has lost the habit of being influenced by the great classics of our country.'

In the chapter 'Kamya Goes Solar' from the book *MBA at 16*, Subroto Bagchi says: 'From Steve Jobs to Harish Hande, from entrepreneurs who build for-profit companies to those who build social enterprises, there is a common streak. All these people are "path creators."' Thus he studies the impact made by visionaries who made innovative efforts to break the vicious cycle of poverty, a very important contribution in a country like ours.

The issue of equality in education preoccupies Nandan Nilekani in 'S Is for Schools: The Challenges in India's Classrooms', an extract from his book *Imagining India*. He talks about the problems our founding fathers faced in formulating an educational policy and the bitter truth that the underprivileged remain so because good schooling continues to stay out of reach for them.

The freedom movement was not only a time of political but also social churning. In his undelivered speech 'Annihilation of Caste' Dr B.R. Ambedkar, the great Dalit icon, explores the issues of power and authority that flow from the hold of religion on people's minds. Thus he, too, takes up the cause of inherited inequality.

There are interesting pieces on animals, too. If you wonder why that royal beast, the lion, is confined to the Gir sanctuary, Valmik Thapar satisfies your curiosity in his account of the history of this magnificent animal in our country, titled 'In the Courts of Emperors' taken from the book *Exotic Aliens*. And if you want to know more about reptiles there is a delightful piece named 'Leave Your Tail and Run' from the book *Cobra in My Kitchen* by the famous snake expert Zai Whitaker. Jim Corbett is known for his inimitable tiger tales, but we have a piece on a more personal note – 'Kunwar Singh' from his book *My India*, in which he has talked about his *shikari* friend Kunwar Singh and the relationship they shared.

We have not forgotten music either. In 'Playing for the Flowers', an extract from Sheila Dhar's riveting memoirs *Raga'n Josh*, the author has sketched a fascinating portrait of a complete musician, Ustad Bundu Khan, the highly respected pre-Partition *sarangi* player. She not only paints a picture of a man completely steeped in his music, but also offers us a glimpse of the lifestyle of a cultured family of the times.

And what about travel? The famous writer Vikram Seth studied for a year in Nanjing University and in 1981 he hitchhiked back to India across four Chinese provinces – Xinjiang (Sinkiang), Gyansu in the north-western desert, the plateau and basin of Qinghai, and finally Tibet, which he was keen to visit. The book *From Heaven Lake: Travels through Sinkiang and Tibet* describes his adventures. He discovered the culture of the diverse ethnic groups he encountered on the way and has written feelingly about the kindness of strangers who helped him at each stage.

Thus, each chapter will engage you with a fresh experience and lead you into a different world. Indeed, we have taken a lot of care to find and select these pieces. Sit back and lose yourself in this multifaceted tour of the best in Indian non-fiction!

Deepa Agarwal
Delhi 2016

A.P.J. ABDUL KALAM

EXTRACT FROM DR KALAM'S AUTOBIOGRAPHY,
WINGS OF FIRE.

'I used to watch cranes and seagulls soar into flight and longed to fly.... Indeed, I *was* the first child from Rameswaram to fly.'

Orientation

Once I settled down at the Schwartz High School, Ramanathapuram, the enthusiastic fifteen-year-old within me re-emerged. My teacher, Iyadurai Solomon, was an ideal guide for an eager young mind that was yet uncertain of the possibilities and alternatives that lay before it. He made his students feel very comfortable in class with his warm and open-minded attitude. He used to say that a good student could learn more from a bad teacher than a poor student from even a skilled teacher.

During my stay at Ramanathapuram, my relationship with him grew beyond that of teacher and pupil. In his company, I learnt that one could exercise enormous influence over the events of one's own life. Iyadurai Solomon used to say, 'To succeed in life and achieve results, you must understand and master three mighty forces – desire, belief, and expectation.' Iyadurai Solomon, who later became a Reverend, taught me that before anything I wanted could happen, I had to desire it intensely and be absolutely certain it would happen. To take an example from my own life, I had been fascinated by the mysteries of the sky and the flight of birds from early childhood. I used to watch cranes and seagulls soar into flight and longed to fly. Simple, provincial boy though I was, I was convinced that one day I, too, would soar up into the skies. Indeed, I *was* the first child from Rameswaram to fly.

Iyadurai Solomon was a great teacher because he instilled in all the children a sense of their own worth. Solomon raised my self-esteem to a high point and convinced me, the son of parents who had not had the benefits of education, that I too could aspire to become whatever I wished. 'With faith, you can change your destiny,' he would say.

One day, when I was in the fourth form, my mathematics teacher, Ramakrishna Iyer, was teaching another class. Inadvertently, I wandered into that classroom and in the manner of an old-fashioned despot, Ramakrishna Iyer caught me by the neck and caned me in front of the whole class. Many months later, when I scored full marks in mathematics, he narrated the incident to the entire school at morning assembly. 'Whomsoever I cane becomes a great man! Take my word, this boy is going to bring glory to his school and to his teachers.' His praise quite made up for the earlier humiliation!

By the time I completed my education at Schwartz, I was a self-confident boy determined to succeed. The decision to go in for further education was taken without a second thought. To us, in those days, the awareness of the possibilities for a professional education did not exist; higher education simply meant going to college. The nearest college was at Tiruchchirappalli, spelled Trichinopoly those days, and called Trichi for short.

In 1950, I arrived at St. Joseph's College, Trichi, to study for the Intermediate examination. I was not a bright student in terms of examination grades but, thanks to my two buddies back in Rameswaram, I had acquired a practical bent of mind.

Whenever I returned to Rameswaram from Schwartz, my elder brother Mustafa Kamal, who ran a provision store on the railway station road, would call me in to give him a little help and then vanish for hours together leaving the shop in my charge. I sold oil, onions, rice and everything else. The fastest moving items, I found, were cigarettes and *bidis*. I used to wonder what made poor people smoke away their hard-earned money. When spared by Mustafa, I would be put in charge of his kiosk by my younger brother, Kasim Mohammed. There I sold novelties made of seashells.

At St. Joseph's, I was lucky to find a teacher like the Rev. Father T.N. Sequeira. He taught us English and was also our hostel warden. We were about a hundred boys living in the three-storeyed hostel building. Rev. Father used to visit each boy every night with a Bible in his hand. His energy and patience was amazing. He was a very considerate person who took care of even the most minute requirements of his students. On Deepavali, on his instructions, the Brother in charge of the hostel and the mess volunteers would visit each room and distribute good gingelly oil for the ritual bath.

I stayed on the St. Joseph's campus for four years and shared my room with two others. One was an orthodox Iyengar from Srirangam and the other a Syrian Christian from Kerala. The three of us had a wonderful time together. When I was made secretary of the vegetarian mess during my third year in the hostel, we invited the Rector, Rev. Father Kalathil, over for lunch one Sunday. Our menu included the choicest preparations from our diverse backgrounds. The result was rather unexpected, but Rev. Father was lavish in his praise of our efforts. We enjoyed every moment with Rev. Father Kalathil, who participated in our unsophisticated conversation with childlike enthusiasm. It was a memorable event for us all.

My teachers at St. Joseph were the true followers of Kanchi Paramacharya, who evoked people to 'enjoy the action of giving'. The vivid memory of our mathematics teachers, Prof Thothathri Iyengar and Prof Suryanarayana Sastry, walking together on the campus inspires me to this day.

When I was in the final year at St. Joseph's, I acquired a taste for English literature. I began to read the great classics, Tolstoy, Scott and Hardy being special favourites despite their exotic settings, and then I moved on to some works in philosophy. It was around this time that I developed a great interest in physics.

The lessons on subatomic physics at St. Joseph's by my physics teachers, Prof Chinna Durai and Prof Krishnamurthy, introduced me to the concept of the half-life period and matters related to the radioactive decay of substances. Sivasubramania Iyer, my science teacher at Rameswaram, had never taught me that most subatomic particles are unstable and that they disintegrate after a certain time into other particles. All this I was learning for the first time. But when he taught me to strive with diligence because decay is inherent in all compounded things, was he not talking of the same thing? I wonder why some people tend to see science as something which takes man away from God. As I look at it, the path of science can always wind through the heart. For me, science has always been the path to spiritual enrichment and self-realization.

Even the rational thought-matrices of science have been home to fairy tales. I am an avid reader of books on cosmology and enjoy reading about celestial bodies. Many friends, while asking me questions related to space flights, sometimes slip into astrology. Quite honestly, I have never really understood the reason behind the great importance attached by people to the faraway planets in our solar system. As an art, I have nothing against astrology, but if it seeks acceptance under the guise of science, I reject it. I do not know how these myths evolved about planets, star constellations, and even satellites – that they can exercise power on human beings. The highly complicated calculations manipulated around the precise movements of celestial bodies, to derive highly subjective conclusions appear illogical to me. As I see it, the Earth is the most powerful and energetic planet. As John Milton puts it so beautifully in *Paradise Lost*, Book VIII:

> . . . *What if the Sun*
> *Be centre to the World, and other Stars . . .*
> *The planet Earth, so steadfast though she seem,*
> *Insensibly three different motions move?*

Wherever you go on this planet, there is movement and life. Even apparently inanimate things like rocks, metal, timber, clay are full of intrinsic movement – with electrons dancing around each nucleus. This motion originates in their response to the confinement imposed on them by the nucleus, by means of electric forces which try to hold them as close as possible. Electrons, just like any individual with a certain amount of energy, detest confinement. The tighter the electrons are held by the nucleus, the higher their orbital velocity will be: in fact, the confinement of electrons in an atom results in enormous velocities of about 1,000 km per second! These high velocities make the atom appear a rigid sphere, just as a fast-moving fan appears like a disc. It is very difficult to compress atoms more strongly – thus giving matter its familiar solid aspect. Everything solid, thus, contains much empty space within and everything stationary contains great movement within. It is as though the great dance of Shiva is being performed on earth during every moment of our existence.

When I joined the B.Sc. degree course at St. Joseph's, I was unaware of any other option for higher education. Nor did I have any information about career opportunities available to a student of science. Only after obtaining a B.Sc. did I realize that physics was not my subject. I had to go into engineering to realize my dreams. I could have joined the Engineering course long ago, right after finishing my Intermediate course. Better late than never, I told myself as I made the detour, applying for admission into the Madras Institute of Technology (MIT), regarded as the crown jewel of technical education in South India at that time.

I managed to be on the list of selected candidates, but admission to this prestigious institution was an expensive affair. Around a thousand rupees was required, and my father could not spare that much money. At that time, my sister, Zohara, stood behind me, mortgaging her gold bangles and chain. I was deeply touched by her determination to see me educated and by her faith in my abilities. I vowed to release her bangles from mortgage with my own earnings. The only way before me to earn money at that point of time was to study hard and get a scholarship. I went ahead at full steam.

What fascinated me most at MIT was the sight of two decommissioned aircraft displayed there for the demonstration of the various subsystems of flying machines. I felt a strange attraction towards them, and would sit near them long after other students had gone back to the hostel, admiring man's will to fly free in the sky, like a bird. After completing my first year, when I had to opt for a specific branch, I almost spontaneously chose aeronautical engineering. The goal was very clear in my mind now; I was going to fly aircraft. I was convinced of this, despite being aware of my lack of assertiveness, which probably came about because of my humble background. Around this time, I made special efforts to try and communicate with different kinds of people. There were setbacks, disappointments and distractions, but my father's inspiring words anchored me in those periods of nebulous drift: 'He who knows others is learned, but the wise one is the one who knows himself. Learning without wisdom is of no use.'

In the course of my education at MIT, three teachers shaped my thinking. Their combined contributions formed the foundation on which I later built my professional career. These three teachers were Prof Sponder, Prof K.A.V. Pandalai and Prof Narasingha Rao. Each one of them had very distinct personalities, but they shared a common impulse – the capacity to feed their students' intellectual hunger by sheer brilliance and untiring zeal.

Prof Sponder taught me technical aerodynamics. He was an Austrian with rich practical experience in aeronautical engineering. During the Second World War, he had been captured by the Nazis and imprisoned in a concentration camp. Understandably, he had developed a very strong dislike for Germans. Incidentally, the aeronautical department was headed by a German, Prof Walter Repenthin. Another well-known professor, Dr Kurt Tank, was a distinguished aeronautical engineer who had designed the German Focke-Wulf Fw 190 single-seater fighter plane, an outstanding combat aircraft of the Second World War. Dr Tank later joined the Hindustan Aeronautics Limited (HAL) in Bangalore and was responsible for the design of India's first jet fighter, the HF-24 Marut.

Notwithstanding these irritants, Prof Sponder preserved his individuality and maintained high professional standards. He was always calm, energetic and in total control of himself. He kept abreast of the latest technologies and expected his students to do the same. I consulted him before opting for aeronautical engineering. He told me that one should never worry about one's future prospects: instead, it was more important to lay sound foundations, to have sufficient enthusiasm and an accompanying passion for one's chosen field of study. The trouble with Indians, Prof Sponder used to observe, was not that they lacked educational opportunities or industrial infrastructure – the trouble was in their failure to discriminate between disciplines and to rationalize their choices. Why aeronautics? Why not electrical engineering? Why not mechanical engineering? I myself would like to tell all novitiate engineering students that when they choose their specialization, the essential point to consider is whether the choice articulates their inner feelings and aspirations.

Prof K.A.V. Pandalai taught me aero-structure design and analysis. He was a cheerful, friendly and enthusiastic teacher, who brought a fresh approach to every year's teaching course. It was Professor Pandalai who opened up the secrets of structural engineering to us. Even today I believe that everyone who has been taught by Prof Pandalai would agree that he was a man of great intellectual integrity and scholarship – but with no trace of arrogance. His students were free to disagree with him on several points in the classroom.

Prof Narasingha Rao was a mathematician, who taught us theoretical aerodynamics. I still remember his method of teaching fluid dynamics. After attending his classes, I began to prefer mathematical physics to any other subject. Often, I have been told I carry a 'surgical knife' to aeronautical design reviews. If it had not been for Prof Rao's kind and persistent advice on picking up proofs to equations of aerodynamic flow, I would not have acquired this metaphorical tool.

Aeronautics is a fascinating subject, containing within it the promise of freedom. The great difference between freedom and escape, between motion and movement, between slide and flow are the secrets of this science. My teachers revealed these truths to me. Through their meticulous teaching, they created within me an excitement about aeronautics. Their intellectual fervour, clarity of thought and passion for perfection helped me to launch into a serious study of fluid dynamics-modes of compressible medium motion, development of shock waves and shock, induced flow separation at increasing speeds, shock stall and shock wave drag.

Slowly, a great amalgamation of information took place in my mind. The structural features of aeroplanes began to gain new meanings – biplanes, monoplanes, tailless planes, canard configured planes, delta-wing planes, all these began to assume increasing significance for me. The three teachers, all of them authorities in their different fields, helped me to mould a composite knowledge.

My third and last year at MIT was a year of transition and was to have a great impact on my later life. In those days, a new climate of political enlightenment and industrial effort was sweeping across the country. I had to test my belief in God and see if it could fit into the matrix of scientific thinking. The accepted view was that a belief in scientific methods was the only valid approach to knowledge. If so, I wondered, was matter alone the ultimate reality and were spiritual phenomena but a manifestation of matter? Were all ethical values relative, and was sensory perception the only source of knowledge and truth? I wondered about these issues, attempting to sort out the vexing question of 'scientific temper' and my own spiritual interests. The value system in which I had been nurtured was profoundly religious. I had been taught that true reality lay beyond the material world in the spiritual realm, and that knowledge could be obtained only through inner experience.

Meanwhile, when I had finished my course work, I was assigned a project to design a low-level attack aircraft together with four other colleagues. I had taken up the responsibility of preparing and drawing the aerodynamic design. My team mates distributed among themselves the tasks of designing the propulsion, structure, control and instrumentation of the aircraft. One day, my design teacher, Prof Srinivasan, then the Director of MIT, reviewed my progress and declared it dismal and disappointing. I offered a dozen excuses for the delay, but none of them impressed Prof Srinivasan. I finally pleaded for a month's time to complete the task. The Professor looked at me for some time and said, 'Look, young man, today is Friday afternoon. I give you three days' time. If by Monday morning I don't get the configuration drawing, your scholarship will be stopped.' I was dumbstruck. The scholarship was my lifeline and I would be quite helpless if it was withdrawn. I could see no other way out but to finish the task as I had been instructed. That night, I remained at the drawing board, skipping dinner. Next morning, I took only an hour's break to freshen up and eat a little food. On Sunday morning, I was very near completion, when suddenly I felt someone else's presence in the room. Prof Srinivasan was watching me from a distance. Coming straight from the gymkhana, he was still in his tennis outfit and had dropped in to see my progress. After examining my work, Prof Srinivasan hugged me affectionately and patted my back in appreciation. He said, 'I knew I was putting you under stress and asking you to meet an impossible deadline. I never expected you to perform so well.'

During the rest of the period of the project, I participated in an essay competition organized by the MIT Tamil Sangam (Literary Society). Tamil is my mother tongue and I am proud of its origins, which have been traced back to Sage Agastya in the pre-Ramayana period; its literature dates back to the fifth century BCE. It is said to be a language moulded by lawyers and grammarians and is internationally acclaimed for its clear-cut logic. I was very enthusiastic about ensuring that science did not remain outside the purview of this wonderful language. I wrote an article entitled 'Let Us Make Our Own Aircraft' in Tamil. The article evoked much interest and I won the competition, taking the first prize from 'Devan', the editor of the popular Tamil weekly, *Ananda Vikatan.*

My most touching memory of MIT is related to Prof Sponder. We were posing for a group photograph as part of a farewell ritual. All the graduating students had lined up in three rows with the professors seated in the front. Suddenly, Prof Sponder got up and looked for me. I was standing in the third row. 'Come and sit with me in the front,' he said. I was taken aback by Prof Sponder's invitation. 'You are my best student and hard work will help you bring a great name for your teachers in future.' Embarrassed by the praise but honoured by the recognition, I sat with Prof Sponder for the photograph. 'Let God be your hope, your stay, your guide and provide the lantern for your feet in your journey into the future,' said the introverted genius, bidding me adieu.

From MIT, I went to Hindustan Aeronautics Limited (HAL) at Bangalore as a trainee. There I worked on engine overhauling as part of a team. Hands-on work on aircraft engine overhauling was very educative. When a principle learnt in the classroom is borne out by practical experience, it creates a strange sense of excitement – akin to unexpectedly running into an old friend among a crowd of strangers. At HAL, I worked on the overhauling of both piston and turbine engines. The hazy concepts of gas dynamics and diffusion processes in the working principle of *after burning* came into sharper focus in my mind. I was also trained in radial engine-cum-drum operations.

I learned how to check a crankshaft for wear and tear, and a connecting rod and crankshaft for twist. I did calibrations of a fixed-pitch fan fitted to a super-charged engine. I opened up pressure and acceleration-cum-speed control systems, and air starter supply systems of turbo-engines. Getting to understand feathering, un-feathering and reversing of propeller engines was very interesting. The demonstration of the delicate art of *beta* (blade angle control) by HAL technicians still lingers in my memory. They had neither studied in major universities, nor were they merely implementing what their engineer-in-charge was suggesting. They had been working hands-on for years and this had given them something like an intuitive feel for the work.

Two alternative opportunities for employment, both close to my long-standing dream of flying, presented themselves before me when I came out of HAL as a graduate aeronautical engineer. One was a career in the Air Force and another was a job at the Directorate of Technical Development and Production, DTD & P (Air), at the Ministry of Defence. I applied for both. The interview calls arrived from both the places almost simultaneously. I was asked to reach Dehradun by the Air Force recruitment authorities and Delhi by DTD & P (Air). The boy from the Coromandel Coast took a train to the North of India. My destination was more than 2,000 km away, and was to be my first encounter with the vastness of my motherland.

BHAGAT SINGH

On April 8, 1929, Bhagat Singh and B.K. Dutt threw a low-intensity bomb in the Central Legislative Assembly 'to make the deaf hear'. The two let themselves be arrested. Through this statement Bhagat Singh emphasized the importance of the motive behind any action.

'Bombs and pistols do not make a revolution. The sword of revolution is honed on the whetstone of ideas.'

Statement before the Lahore High Court Bench

MY LORDS,

Neither are we lawyers nor masters of the English language, nor are we holders of degrees. Therefore, please do not expect any declamatory speech from us. We pray that instead of going into the errors of language in our statement, Your Lordships will try to grasp its real sense.

I will let our lawyers talk about other points, and focus on one point only. This point is very significant in our case. The point is about what our intentions were and to what extent we are guilty. This is a very complicated question and no one will be able to express to you the height of the mental exaltation that motivated us to think and act in a particular manner. We wish that this should be kept in mind while assessing our intentions and our offence. According to the famous jurist Solomon, one should not be punished for a criminal offence if one's aim is not against the law.

We had submitted a written statement in the Sessions Court. That statement explains our aim and, as such, explains our intentions also. But the learned judge dismissed it with one stroke of the pen, saying that 'generally the operation of law is not affected by how or why one committed the offence. In this country the aim of the offence is very rarely mentioned in legal commentaries.'

My Lords, our argument is that under the circumstances the learned judge ought to have judged us either by the result of our action or on the basis of the psychological aspect of our statement. But he did not take any of these factors into account.

The main point to be considered is that the two bombs we threw in the Assembly did not injure anyone either physically or financially. However, the punishment awarded to us is not only overly harsh but vindictive as well. Furthermore, the motive of the offence of an accused cannot be discovered without knowing his psychology. And no one can do justice to an accused without taking his motive into consideration. If we ignore the motive, the greatest generals of the world will appear to be ordinary murderers; revenue officers will appear the same as thieves and cheats. Even judges will be blamed for murder. In this manner the whole social system and the civilization will be reduced to murders, thefts and cheating. If we overlook the motive, the government will have no right to expect any sacrifices from its people and its officials. Ignore the motive and every religious preacher will be labelled a preacher of lies, and every prophet will be charged with leading crores of simple and ignorant people astray.

If we disregard the motive, then Jesus Christ will appear to be a man responsible for creating disorder, destroying peace and preaching rebellion, and will be considered a 'dangerous personality' in the language of the law. But we worship him. He commands great respect in our hearts and his image arouses spiritual feelings in us. Why? Because his actions were inspired by a high ideal. The rulers of that age could not recognize that great idealism. They only saw his external actions. Nineteen centuries have passed since then. Have we not progressed during this period? Shall we repeat that mistake? If yes, then we shall have to admit that all the sacrifices mankind has made and all the struggles of the great martyrs were of no use and it would seem that we have remained at the same place where we stood twenty centuries back.

From the legal point of view too, the question of motive is of particular importance. Take the example of General Dyer. He took the decision of firing at unarmed people and killed hundreds of innocent men, women and children. But the military court did not order him to be shot. It gave him lakhs of rupees as an award. Take another example. Shri Kharag Bahadur Singh, a young Gurkha, killed a Marwari in Calcutta. If the motive were to be set aside, then Kharag Bahadur Singh ought to have been hanged. But he was awarded a mild sentence of only a few years. He was even released much before the expiry of his sentence. Was there any loophole in the law that helped him escape capital punishment? Or, was the charge of murder not proved against him? Like us, he too accepted the full responsibility of his action, but he escaped death. He is a free man today. I ask Your Lordship, why was he not awarded capital punishment? His action was well calculated and well planned. From the motive point of view, his action was more serious and damaging than ours. He was awarded a mild punishment because his intentions were good. He saved society from a foul leech who had sucked the lifeblood of so many pretty young girls. Kharag Singh was given a mild punishment simply to uphold the formalities of the law.

This principle (that the law does not take motive into consideration) is quite absurd. This is against the basic principles of law, which declares that 'the law is for man and not man for the law'. Then, why are the same norms not being applied in our case too? It is quite clear that while convicting Kharag Singh, his motive was kept in mind, otherwise a murderer can never escape the hangman's noose. Are we being deprived of the ordinary benefit of the law because our offence is against the government, or because our action is of political importance?

My Lords, under these circumstances, please permit us to assert that a government that hides behind such callous methods has no right to exist. If it is exists, it is for a passing time only, and that too with the blood of thousands on its head. If the law does not examine the motive, there can be no justice, nor can there be a stable peace.

Mixing arsenic (poison) in flour will not be considered a crime, if its purpose is to kill rats. But if the purpose is to kill a man, it becomes a crime of murder. Therefore, such laws that do not stand the test of reason and that are against the principle of justice, should be abolished. It is because of such unjust laws that many great intellectuals have had to adopt the path of revolt.

The facts of our case are very simple. We threw two bombs in the Legislative Assembly on April 8, 1929. As a result of the explosion, a few people received minor scratches. There was pandemonium in the chamber, hundreds of visitors and members of the Assembly ran out. Only my friend B.K. Dutt and I remained seated in the visitors' gallery and gave ourselves up for arrest. We were tried for attempt to murder, and convicted for life. As mentioned above, as a result of the bomb explosion, only four or five persons were slightly injured and one bench got damaged. We offered ourselves for arrest without any resistance. The Sessions Judge admitted that we could have very easily escaped, had we had any intention of doing that. We accepted our offence and gave a statement explaining our position. We are not afraid of punishment, but we do not wish to be understood wrongly. The judge removed a few paragraphs from our statement. This we consider to be detrimental to clarifying our correct position.

A proper examination of the full text of our statement will make it clear that, according to us, our country is passing through a difficult phase. We caught sight of the impending catastrophe and thought it right to give a timely warning in a loud voice, and we gave the warning in the manner we thought right. We may be wrong. Our line of thinking and that of the learned judge may be different, but that does not mean that we should be deprived of the permission to express our ideas, and wrong ideas be propagated in our name.

In our statement we explained in detail what we mean by 'Long Live Revolution' and 'Down with Imperialism'. That formed the crux of our thinking. That portion was removed from our statement. Generally, an incorrect meaning is attributed to the word revolution. That is not our understanding. Bombs and pistols do not make a revolution. The sword of revolution is honed on the whetstone of ideas. This is what we wished to emphasize. By revolution we mean the end of the sorrows of capitalist wars. It was not appropriate to pronounce judgement without understanding our aims and objectives, and the process of achieving them. To associate erroneous ideas with our names is absolute injustice.

It was essential to give a warning in time, that the unrest of the people is growing and that the troubles may take a serious turn, if not addressed quickly and suitably. If our warning is not heeded, no human power will be able to stop it. We took this step to give proper direction to the storm. We are serious students of history. We believe that, had the ruling powers acted correctly at the appropriate time, there would have been no bloody revolutions in France and Russia. Several great powers of the world tried to control the storm of ideas and were drowned in bloodshed instead. The rulers cannot change the flow of the current. We wished to sound the first warning. Had we aimed at killing important personalities, we would have failed to fulfill our aim.

My Lords, this was the aim and the spirit behind our action, and the result of the action corroborates our statement. There is one more point that needs clarification, and that is regarding the strength of the bombs. Had we no idea of the power of the bombs, there would have been no question of our throwing them in the presence of our respected national leaders like Pandit Motilal Nehru, Shri Kelkar, Shri Jayakar and Shri Jinnah. How could we have risked the lives of our leaders? After all, we are not insane and, were we so, we would have surely been sent to the lunatic asylum, instead of being put in jail. We had complete knowledge of the strength of the bombs and that is why we acted with so much confidence. It would have been very easy to have thrown the bombs on the occupied benches, but it was more difficult to throw them on unoccupied seats. Were we not of saner mind or had we been mentally unbalanced, the bombs would have fallen on occupied benches and not in empty areas. Therefore I would say that we should be rewarded for the courage we displayed in carefully selecting the empty places. Under these conditions, My Lords, we think we have not been understood correctly. We have not come before you to get our sentences reduced. We have come here to clarify our position. We wish that we should not receive any unjust treatment, nor should any unjust opinion be pronounced on our actions. The question of punishment is of secondary importance to us.

BHIMRAO RAMJI AMBEDKAR

EXTRACT FROM *ANNIHILATION OF CASTE: THE ANNOTATED CRITICAL EDITION* – A PASSIONATE COMMENTARY ON THE DEVASTATING EFFECTS OF CASTE IN HINDU SOCIETY.

'The caste system is not merely a division of labour. *It is also a division of labourers.*'

From an Undelivered Speech, 1936

Can the socialists ignore the problem arising out of the social order? The socialists of India,[1] following their fellows in Europe, are seeking to apply the economic interpretation of history to the facts of India. They propound that man is an economic creature, that his activities and aspirations are bound by economic facts, that property is the only source of power. They therefore preach that political and social reforms are but gigantic illusions, and that economic reform by equalization of property must have precedence over every other kind of reform. One may join issue with every one of these premises – on which rests the socialists' case for economic reform as having priority over every other kind of reform. One may contend that the economic motive is not the only motive by which man is actuated. That economic power is the only kind of power, no student of human society can accept.

That the social status of an individual by itself often becomes a source of power and authority is made clear by the sway which the Mahatmas have held over the common man. Why do millionaires in India obey penniless sadhus and fakirs? Why do millions of paupers in India sell their trifling trinkets which constitute their only wealth, and go to Benares and Mecca? That religion is the source of power is illustrated by the history of India, where the priest holds sway over the common man often greater than that of the magistrate, and where everything, even such things as strikes and elections, so easily takes a religious turn and can so easily be given a religious twist.

Take the case of the plebeians of Rome as a further illustration of the power of religion over man. It throws great light on this point. The plebeians had fought for a share in the supreme executive under the Roman Republic, and had secured the appointment of a plebeian consul elected by a separate electorate constituted by the Comitia Centuriata,[2] which was an assembly of plebeians. They wanted a consul of their own because they felt that the patrician consuls used to discriminate against the plebeians in carrying on the administration. They had apparently obtained a great gain, because under the republican constitution of Rome one consul had the power of vetoing an act of the other consul.

But did they in fact gain anything? The answer to this question must be in the negative. The plebeians never could get a plebeian consul who could be said to be a strong man, and who could act independently of the patrician consul. In the ordinary course of things the plebeians should have got a strong plebeian consul, in view of the fact that his election was to be by a separate electorate of plebeians. The question is, why did they fail in getting a strong plebeian to officiate as their consul?

The answer to this question reveals the dominion which religion exercises over the minds of men. It was an accepted creed of the whole Roman populus that no official could enter upon the duties of his office unless the Oracle of Delphi[3] declared that he was acceptable to the goddess. The priests who were in charge of the temple of the goddess of Delphi were all patricians. Whenever therefore the plebeians elected a consul who was known to be a strong party man and opposed to the patricians – or 'communal', to use the term that is current in India – the Oracle invariably declared that he was not acceptable to the goddess. This is how the plebeians were cheated out of their rights.

But what is worthy of note is that the plebeians permitted themselves to be thus cheated because they, too, like the patricians, held firmly the belief that the approval of the goddess was a condition precedent to the taking charge by an official of his duties, and that election by the people was not enough. If the plebeians had contended that election was enough and that the approval by the goddess was not necessary, they would have derived the fullest benefit from the political right which they had obtained. But they did not. They agreed to elect another, less suitable to themselves but more suitable to the goddess – which in fact meant more amenable to the patricians. Rather than give up religion, the plebeians gave up the material gain for which they had fought so hard. Does this not show that religion can be a source of power as great as money, if not greater?

The fallacy of the socialists[4] lies in supposing that because in the present stage of European society property as a source of power is predominant, the same is true of India, or the same was true of Europe in the past. Religion, social status and property are all sources of power and authority which one man has to control the liberty of another. One is predominant at one stage; the other is predominant at another stage. That is the only difference. If liberty is the ideal, and if liberty means the destruction of the dominion which one man holds over another, then obviously it cannot be insisted upon that economic reform must be the one kind of reform worthy of pursuit. If the source of power and dominion is, at any given time or in any given society, social and religious, then social reform and religious reform must be accepted as the necessary sort of reform.

One can thus attack the doctrine of economic interpretation of history adopted by the socialists of India. But I recognize that the economic interpretation of history is not necessary for the validity of the socialist contention that equalization of property is the only real reform and that it must precede everything else. However, what I would like to ask the socialists is this: Can you have economic reform without first bringing about a reform of the social order? The socialists of India do not seem to have considered this question.[5] I do not wish to do them an injustice. I give below a quotation from a letter which a prominent socialist wrote a few days ago to a friend of mine, in which he said, 'I do not believe that we can build up a free society in India so long as there is a trace of this ill-treatment and suppression of one class by another. Believing as I do in a socialist ideal, inevitably I believe in perfect equality in the treatment of various classes and groups. I think that socialism offers the only true remedy for this as well as other problems.'

Now the question that I would like to ask is: Is it enough for a socialist to say, 'I believe in perfect equality in the treatment of the various classes?' To say that such a belief is enough is to disclose a complete lack of understanding of what is involved in socialism. If socialism is a practical programme and is not merely an ideal, distant and far off, the question for a socialist is not whether he believes in equality. The question for him is whether he minds one class ill-treating and suppressing another class as a matter of system, as a matter of principle – and thus allow tyranny and oppression to continue to divide one class from another.

Let me analyze the factors that are involved in the realization of socialism in order to explain fully my point. Now it is obvious that the economic reform contemplated by the socialists cannot come about unless there is a revolution resulting in the seizure of power. That seizure of power must be by a proletariat. The first question I ask is: Will the proletariat of India combine to bring about this revolution? What will move men to such an action? It seems to me that, other things being equal, the only thing that will move one man to take such an action is the feeling of equality and fraternity and – above all – of justice. Men will not join in a revolution for the equalization of property unless they know that after the revolution is achieved they will be treated equally, and that there will be no discrimination of caste and creed.

The assurance of a socialist leading the revolution that he does not believe in caste, I am sure, will not suffice. The assurance must be the assurance proceeding from a much deeper foundation – namely, the mental attitude of the compatriots towards one another in their spirit of personal equality and fraternity. Can it be said that the proletariat of India, poor as it is, recognizes no distinctions except that of the rich and the poor? Can it be said that the poor in India recognize no such distinctions of caste or creed, high or low? If the fact is that they do, what unity of front can be expected from such a proletariat in its action against the rich? How can there be a revolution if the proletariat cannot present a united front?

Suppose for the sake of argument that by some freak of fortune a revolution does take place and the socialists come into power, will they not have to deal with the problems created by the particular social order prevalent in India? I can't see how a socialist state in India can function for a second without having to grapple with the problems created by the prejudices which make Indian people observe the distinctions of high and low, clean and unclean. If socialists are not to be content with the mouthing of fine phrases, if the socialists wish to make socialism a definite reality, then they must recognize that the problem of social reform is fundamental, and that for them there is no escape from it.

That the social order prevalent in India is a matter which a socialist must deal with; that unless he does so he cannot achieve his revolution; and that if he does achieve it as a result of good fortune, he will have to grapple with the social order if he wishes to realize his ideal – is a proposition which in my opinion is incontrovertible. He will be compelled to take account of caste after the revolution, if he does not take account of it before the revolution. This is only another way of saying that, turn in any direction you like caste is the monster that crosses your path. You cannot have political reform, you cannot have economic reform, unless you kill this monster.

It is a pity that caste even today has its defenders. The defences are many. It is defended on the ground that the caste system is but another name for division of labour; and if division of labour is a necessary feature of every civilized society, then it is argued that there is nothing wrong in the caste system. Now the first thing that is to be urged against this view is that the caste system is not merely a division of labour. *It is also a division of labourers.*[6] Civilized society undoubtedly needs division of labour. But in no civilized society is division of labour accompanied by this unnatural division of labourers into watertight compartments. The caste system is not merely a division of labourers – which is quite different from division of labour – it is a hierarchy in which the divisions of labourers are graded one above the other. In no other country is the division of labour accompanied by this gradation of labourers.

There is also a third point of criticism against this view of the caste system. This division of labour is not spontaneous; it is not based on natural aptitudes. Social and individual efficiency requires us to develop the capacity of an individual to the point of competency to choose and to make his own career. This principle is violated in the caste system, in so far as it involves an attempt to appoint tasks to individuals in advance – selected not on the basis of trained original capacities, but on that of the social status of the parents.[7]

Looked at from another point of view, this stratification of occupations which is the result of the caste system is positively pernicious. Industry is never static.[8] It undergoes rapid and abrupt changes. With such changes, an individual must be free to change his occupation. Without such freedom to adjust himself to changing circumstances, it would be impossible for him to gain his livelihood. Now the caste system will not allow Hindus to take to occupations where they are wanted, if they do not belong to them by heredity. If a Hindu is seen to starve rather than take to new occupations not assigned to his caste, the reason is to be found in the caste system. By not permitting readjustment of occupations, caste becomes a direct cause of much of the unemployment we see in the country.

As a form of division of labour, the caste system suffers from another serious defect. The division of labour brought about by the caste system is not a division based on choice. Individual sentiment, individual preference, has no place in it. It is based on the dogma of predestination. Considerations of social efficiency would compel us to recognize that the greatest evil in the industrial system is not so much poverty and the suffering that it involves, as the fact that so many persons have callings which make no appeal to those who are engaged in them. Such callings constantly provoke one to aversion, ill will and the desire to evade.[9]

There are many occupations in India which, on account of the fact that they are regarded as degraded by the Hindus, provoke those who are engaged in them to aversion. There is a constant desire to evade and escape from such occupations, which arises solely because of the blighting effect which they produce upon those who follow them, owing to the slight and stigma cast upon them by the Hindu religion. What efficiency can there be in a system under which neither men's hearts nor their minds are in their work? As an economic organization caste is therefore a harmful institution, inasmuch as it involves the subordination of man's natural powers and inclinations to the exigencies of social rules.

Some have dug a biological trench in defence of the caste system. It is said that the object of caste was to preserve purity of race and purity of blood. Now ethnologists[10] are of the opinion that men of pure race exist nowhere and that there has been a mixture of all races in all parts of the world. Especially is this the case with the people of India. Mr D.R. Bhandarkar in his paper on 'Foreign Elements in the Hindu Population' has stated that 'There is hardly a class or caste in India which has not a foreign strain in it. There is an admixture of alien blood not only among the warrior classes – the Rajputs and the Marathas – but also among the Brahmins who are under the happy delusion that they are free from all foreign elements.'[11] The caste system cannot be said to have grown as a means of preventing the admixture of races, or as a means of maintaining purity of blood.

As a matter of fact the caste system came into being long after the different races of India had commingled in blood and culture.[12] To hold that distinctions of castes are really distinctions of race, and to treat different castes as though they were so many different races, is a gross perversion of facts.

DILIP SALWI

EXTRACT FROM *REMEMBERING OUR LEADERS.*

'He was the man who placed India on the world map of science.'

C.V. Raman

In recent years, February 28 is celebrated as National Science Day all over India. On this day, scientists give talks on the latest developments in science and technology to the common man and children; films, videos and TV features concerning science and technology are shown; functions and exhibitions about scientific progress are held; and awards and prizes for contributions to science and technology are given.

Why has this particular day been selected to bring developments in science and technology into national focus?

Way back in 1928, a major discovery in science was made on this day in the country, with simple, inexpensive equipment. The entire world woke up to the fact that even scientifically backward, British-ruled India could make a fundamental contribution to the realm of modern science. It was a milestone in the history of India because the same discovery soon fetched the Nobel Prize for its discoverer. It was equally a milestone in the march of science.

National Science Day is a reminder of the epochal event that all Indians are proud of and still look upon with admiration and affection. That major discovery was what is today known as the Raman Effect. It was discovered by C.V. Raman in the laboratory of the Indian Association for the Cultivation of Science, Calcutta.* He was the man who placed India on the world map of science. After 60 years of the discovery, the Raman Effect is being used as an extremely refined tool to study solids, liquids and gases in modern laboratories across the world.

Interest in Science

Chandrasekhara Venkata Raman was born on November 7, 1888, near Tiruchchirappalli, Tamil Nadu. His father was a teacher in a college, with a meagre salary of ten rupees. He loved reading books and had a small library in his house. So, from a tender age, Raman was introduced to books on science and English classics. His appreciation of music, which later became the subject of his scientific investigations, also began at an early age. He would watch his father play the *veena* for hours together.

When his father shifted to the coastal town of Visakhapatanam, Raman's school was situated on the seashore. The expanse of the blue sea could be seen through the windows of his classroom. It captured the boy's imagination and later became the subject of his studies.

Physics fascinated him at an early age. Once he built an electric dynamo from scratch. On another occasion, when he was ill, he would not go to sleep until his father demonstrated the utility of the Leyden Jar!

* *Now Kolkata.*

In the class, Raman was an extremely bright student and used to win prizes and scholarships. The teachers often used to praise his grasp of English, his independent nature and strength of character. Some called him the best student they ever had! He was hardly eleven when he stood first in the Matriculation examination.

On the first day at the Presidency College, Madras, the European teacher was surprised to see little Raman in his class and enquired whether he was there by mistake!

When Raman did M.A., he hardly attended the classes. Professor R.L. Jones knew he could look after himself and allowed Raman to pursue his own interests. Most often Raman would be busy conducting scientific investigations in the college laboratory. He would use the Professor's Fabry–Perot Interferometer to conduct measurements of light rays.

Imagine Raman's bent of mind at that age when scientific investigations were not even known in the country. Moreover, he went on to discover something that was not mentioned in the available books. Even Professor Jones could not explain what had been discovered. He suggested to Raman to write down his findings in the form of a research paper and send it to *The Philosophical Magazine* published in London. His paper was promptly published in the November 1906 issue of the magazine. It was Raman's first contribution to science. He was then 18 years old.

Soon Raman wrote another research paper and sent it to the internationally reputed science journal *Nature*, London. He had by then developed the self-confidence to conduct scientific investigations on his own. Raman sent a letter to Lord Rayleigh, the most respected British scientist of the time, asking some questions about his scientific investigations. Lord Rayleigh wrote back addressing him as Professor! How could he have imagined that a teenaged Indian boy was conducting scientific investigations?

Indeed, Raman's genius was unmatched!

His teachers persuaded Raman's father to send him to England for higher studies. Raman would have sailed for England and would have been lost to the country like countless others but for the objection of a British medical officer. The doctor found Raman's health too delicate to stand the rigours of the English climate. Raman had no option then but to sit for a competitive examination conducted by the British Government to recruit staff. He was selected as an officer in the Finance Department of the government.

Raman took up the government job that fetched him a good salary and a bungalow. He married Lokasundari.

Research Work

Any other person would have happily settled down in life. But how could Raman give up science? It was his passion. He built a small laboratory at home and conducted investigations of subjects that interested him.

Raman's young wife cooperated with him in all his investigations and kept him free to concentrate on his scientific work. She believed she was destined to serve Raman. She was indeed the woman behind the great man that Raman became.

In 1907, Raman was transferred to Calcutta, the then Mecca of science. Not more than a week had passed, when travelling from home to office in a tram car, he noticed the signboard of the Indian Association for the Cultivation of

Science, on Bowbazar Street. He rushed to the office of the Association the same evening. The Association was the pioneering institute built by Dr Mahendra Lal Sirkar in 1876, to conduct scientific investigations in the country. For various reasons, the building of the Association was, however, only being used as a meeting place for men interested in science and for occasional popular science lectures. The laboratory and equipment of the Association lay mostly unused. When Raman showed a keen desire to conduct scientific investigations in the laboratory, the instruments and equipment were placed at his disposal. Thus began Raman's scientific investigations at the Association, which eventually led to his Nobel-Prize-winning discovery.

Raman would reach the laboratory of the Association at 5.30 a.m. everyday and return by 7.45 a.m. to get ready for the office. Again, after office hours, he would be in the laboratory around 5 p.m. and stay up to 10 p.m. Even on Sundays he would be in the laboratory. This was his routine for several years.

Raman's scientific investigations were then mostly confined to musical instruments. He found out why musical instruments like the *veena, mridangam* and *tabla* made melodious sounds.

In his investigations, Raman took the assistance of Ashutosh Dey, a lay member of the Association. He trained Dey so well in scientific investigations that later he (Dey) could write his own findings, which duly appeared in prestigious science journals. This showed Raman's faith in people who wanted to learn rather than those who had simply been trained or taught. In fact, he soon built a team of young men who would participate in his investigations.

He also began to give popular lectures on science in the hall of the Association, to bring the latest developments in science to young people. He became a sort of spokesman for science in the country.

Raman's activities for science impressed Sir Ashutosh Mukherjee, the 'Tiger of Bengal', the Vice-Chancellor of the Calcutta University. He requested the British Government to relieve Raman of his services for two years so that he could pursue his scientific interests wholeheartedly. But the Government did not agree. Meanwhile, the Taraknath Palit Chair of Physics was established at the Association. It was to be offered to a distinguished scientist. Mukherjee was keen that Raman should take up the Chair but he did not fulfil one essential condition. He had not worked abroad. Mukherjee suggested to Raman to do so but the scientist refused. He requested Mukherjee to overrule that condition if his services were required. Eventually, Mukherjee persuaded himself to do that. Raman resigned from the lucrative government job to take up the Palit Chair of Physics at the Association in 1917. It meant considerable loss in power and salary but Raman was ready to give up everything for science.

'This one instance encourages me to entertain hope that there would be no lack of seekers after truth in the Temple of Knowledge which it is our ambition to erect,' remarked Mukherjee, admiring Raman's sacrifice. Thereafter, Raman became a full-time scientist.

Fond of Teaching

In addition to scientific investigations, Raman had to teach the students. There was, however, no time restriction for him. Most of the time, even after dinner he would be in the Association building, talking to the students, encouraging them and guiding them in their scientific investigations. He also took up scientific investigations in other subjects like light phenomena, X-rays, magnetism and crystals. In fact, he got a door built between his residence and the laboratory so that he could be easily available to anyone.

In 1921, Raman was invited to attend the Universities Congress held at Oxford, England. It became a turning point in his career. Often, a sea voyage makes itself monotonous because there is nothing much to see except the sea and the sky. For Raman, however, the sea and the sky became not monotonous but a subject of scientific interest. The deep blue of the Mediterranean Sea especially attracted his attention. He began to wonder what made it so.

Raman knew that Lord Rayleigh had attributed the blue of the sky to the light rays of the sun scattered by the molecules of nitrogen and oxygen in the air. Lord Rayleigh had also claimed that the blue of the sea was a mere reflection of the blue sky. But on seeing the deep blue of the Mediterranean, Raman was dissatisfied with the simple explanation. Standing on the deck of the ship, he decided to investigate. He rushed downstairs to his cabin and brought up a small instrument to test whether the deep blue of the sea was reflected light or not. He found that the deep blue colour came from within the sea! Thrilled, he decided to pursue this line of investigation in his laboratory at Calcutta.

Raman always asked 'Why' whenever he saw some natural phenomenon. This is the hallmark of a scientist. Even while sightseeing in London he conducted simple experiments in the famous Whispering Galleries!

Back in Calcutta, Raman took up the study of scattering of light by molecules of sea water, then various types of liquids, solids and gases. In due course, he found that the blue of the sea was mainly due to the scattering of blue light by the molecules of sea water when sunlight fell on them. The rest of the colours of the sunlight were absorbed.

The investigations brought him applause from all over the world. He also built a team of workers who exclusively pursued such studies. For his contributions to this field of science called 'Optics', Raman was elected Fellow of the Royal Society, London, in 1924. It was a high honour for any scientist. At the dinner given in honour of Raman, Ashutosh Mukherjee asked him, 'What next?' Pat came the reply, 'Nobel Prize!'

To many attending the dinner it might have then sounded like an empty boast because science had but begun in the British-ruled India. Who could have dreamt that an Indian could win a Nobel Prize in science so soon? But Raman was serious about it. 'Ambition, courage and endeavour' were his watchwords. His ambition was to win the Nobel Prize, and he was also prepared to put his heart and soul into his scientific investigations. Unfortunately, Mukherjee did not live long enough to see Raman bag the Nobel Prize.

It was while Raman and his students were investigating the scattering of light by the molecules of liquids that the inklings of the Raman Effect were observed. A fine slit permitted a beam of sunlight to pass through a liquid chemical, like benzene. The scattered light – the spectrum – was observed at the other end with the help of a Direct Vision Spectroscope. The scattered beam appeared like a line of lines as the sunlight came through a fine slit. In addition to these lines, Raman and his students observed some unusual lines in the spectrum. They thought the lines were due to impurities present in the liquid chemical. Howsoever they purified the chemical, the lines persisted! With other liquid chemicals also, the lines were seen.

For some years, investigations on the lines continued. These did not produce any result. Raman wondered ever what could they be. Once he supposed they were due to the particle nature of light which was then being talked about. Those were the early days of modern physics. That light behaves like a wave as well as a particle was a new theory.

The Raman Effect

In 1927 the Nobel Prize in physics was awarded to A.H. Compton of the University of Chicago, USA, for his discovery of the Compton Effect. In the case of the Compton Effect, unusual lines were observed when X-rays (a form of electromagnetic radiation like light) passed through a material. The Compton Effect was produced owing to the particle nature of X-rays. Raman rightly thought something similar was also happening in his experiments.

The light beam was behaving like a stream of particles – photons. The photons were hitting the molecules of the chemical liquid, say, like a cricket ball hitting a football. The cricket ball hit the football hard but all it could do was to move it a little. The cricket ball itself rebounded or went off in another direction with lesser energy, having lost some of it to the football. The unusual lines occurred because some photons lost their energy in this manner and so appeared at a different point in the spectrum of scattered light. The other photons were simply deflected off their path without gain or loss in their energy and so appeared in their normal position in the spectrum.

The loss in the energy of the photons and the resulting unusual lines in the spectrum was the Raman Effect.

The amount of energy lost by the photons gives information on the molecules of the liquid chemical that scattered them. Different molecules interact differently with the photons, losing varied amounts of energy, like a cricket ball would on colliding with, say, a tennis ball, a golf ball or a football. By measuring the energy loss of photons from the unusual Raman lines, the internal arrangement of molecules of liquids, solids or gases could be ascertained. The Raman Effect could thus become a useful tool to understand the internal structure of matter. Raman and his students determined how molecules were arranged in various types of optical glasses, crystals of different substances, gemstones, pearls, diamonds, quartz; in liquid compounds such as benzene, toluene, pentane, and in compressed gases such as carbon dioxide and nitrous oxide.

Before Raman announced his discovery, he wanted to be sure. To observe the unusual lines more clearly, he substituted a powerful mercury vapour lamp for sunlight. Indeed, the lines became more prominent. He became absolutely sure of the new discovery. That was on February 28, 1928. The next day the scientist announced it to the foreign press. The prestigious *Nature* published it. On March 16, Raman gave a talk on his discovery, New Radiation, to the South Indian Science Association at Bangalore. The first confirmation of the effect came from

R.W. Wood of John Hopkins University, USA. Soon, all the major laboratories of the world took up the investigation of the Raman Effect. It became an additional support of the newly emerging modern physics.

Nobel Prize

We may imagine the popularity and utility of the Raman Effect from the fact that within ten years of its discovery, about 2,000 research papers were published about it the world over. It was mainly utilized to determine the internal molecular structure of different solids, liquids and gases.

Honours were bestowed on Raman. He was but forty-two. So sure was Raman of winning the Nobel Prize for his discovery that he booked two passages to Stockholm a few months before the prizes were announced in December 1930!

Raman was the first Asian and non-white to win the Nobel Prize in science. It was a moment of great pride for every Indian. It showed that Indians were in no way inferior to Europeans in the field of science, which in those days were believed to be theirs.

Earlier, Rabindranath Tagore had won the 1913 Nobel Prize for literature.

Following the Nobel Prize, several other prestigious honours came to Raman from different parts of the world. The recognition gave a big fillip to science in the country. The achievement was indeed historic. Young boys and girls were inspired to take science in those pre-Independence days of India.

In 1933, Raman was appointed Director of the Indian Institute of Science, Bangalore, another of the country's premier scientific organizations. Here he started a new Department of Physics, for none existed. Again he began to build a team of young scientists to conduct scientific investigations. He made changes in the Institute's rules and regulations so that scientists could pursue enquiries without hitch or botheration about worldly things. Sometimes, he even used to pay money from his own pocket to expedite the investigations.

In due course, Raman founded the Indian Academy of Sciences, and elected scientists as its Fellows who had made a mark through their contributions. Annual meetings of the Academy were held in different cities and towns so that local young votaries could attend them and exchange views with the scientists. This was one method of attracting the young to science, Raman thought. He himself used to give popular lectures on the latest developments in science to urge them to take up scientific investigations. He saw to it that promising young scientists also got proper jobs and positions in universities and institutes in the country.

How a science movement could be started in India was always uppermost in Raman's mind. He was ever on the look out for opportunities in this direction. One such opportunity came when the Jewish scientists in Germany were persecuted under Hitler's Nazi regime and were seeking asylum in other countries. Raman invited some top physicists like Max Born, Erwin Schrodinger and others to settle down in our country so that their very presence would trigger off scientific investigations. But the management of the Indian Institute of Science could not appreciate Raman's vision. As a result, Raman gave up the directorship. The management did not share Raman's scientific foresight. This was a pity, since we know how science, recognizing no barriers, has taken countries forward, and helped humanity's advance. Shortly, after his resignation, Raman was offered the directorship of a prestigious science institute in Holland, which he flatly declined. He was keen to stay in the country itself and create for it a science base.

The Research Institute

In 1948, Raman realized his dream of building his own institute, now known as the Raman Research Institute, at Bangalore. He gathered his own savings, asked for donations and also started some industries to provide a regular source of funds for running the Institute.

The Institute reflected Raman's aesthetic tastes. It had a garden-like air with blooming bougainvilleas, jacarandas and roses and also a wide variety of trees from eucalyptus to mahogany. Here, Raman conducted scientific investigations on subjects that interested him. Anything that sparkled or shone became a subject of his investigations. In fact, he bought about 300 diamonds – king of solids – and conducted studies on their internal structure and physical properties. Even coloured feathers of birds, butterflies, beetles and flower petals caught his attention. He conducted investigations as to why they were so colourful. As a result of his studies, he forwarded a theory of vision and colour and put down his investigations in a book *The Physiology of Vision*. It is only in recent times that this subject is attracting the attention of scientists. He always knew how to dig out new avenues of investigation different from those taken up in the West.

After India attained Independence in 1947, Raman felt disappointed as he found no effort was being made to evolve science in the country itself, something which he had been trying to do all the time. Instead, scientists were sent abroad for higher studies in large numbers. The country itself offered much scope for scientific studies, and it was in any case our duty to build up the infrastructure. We needed to look within.

To set an example to young scientists not to hanker after foreign degrees and honours, he himself resigned from the Fellowship of the Royal Society, London. He developed a contempt for politicization of science; he felt politics and science could rarely go together. The latter would suffer and be baulked. Even when he was sounded for the Vice-Presidentship of India, a high honour, Raman declined the offer without a second thought. In1954, he became the first scientist to be conferred with the rare title of Bharat Ratna.

A Visionary

For several years Raman remained a recluse. But Raman was nothing if not restless. He enjoyed the company of children. He would invite schoolchildren to the Institute and spend hours showing them around the place. He took great pains to make them understand the working of his equipment and the kind of investigations he conducted. He would also visit schools and give lectures on science. He would often tell children that science had to be found in the world and not simply in laboratories, that they should see stars, flowers and other phenomena that occurred around them, ask questions regarding them, and use their intelligence and science to find their answers.

Several present-day eminent scientists took up science after listening to his lectures. He was indeed the herald of a new dawn.

Chandrasekhara Venkata Raman lived long enough to see a revival of interest in the Raman Effect in the modern laboratories of the world, thanks to the invention of laser, a highly coherent and powerful light, in 1960. Earlier, it used to take several days to get a clear picture of the Raman Effect. Laser produced the same result within seconds. The Raman Effect is, therefore, increasingly being employed to analyze chemicals present in minute quantities in various fields, namely, chemical industries, pollution studies, pharmaceutical industries and biological studies. It is able to give information on things never thought of when Raman discovered the Effect.

On November 21,1970, after a brief illness at the age of 82, C.V. Raman passed away.

Raman was the first to put India on the consciousness of the modern scientific world. C.V. Raman picked up a lost thread, and the principles he proclaimed illumined the path, as it were, for a free India to take for its growth and strength. The fillip that Raman gave to India's recovery and upsurge of science is immeasurable.

JAWAHARLAL NEHRU

EXTRACT FROM *LETTERS FROM A FATHER TO HIS DAUGHTER* – A COLLECTION OF LETTERS WRITTEN TO INDIRA GANDHI IN 1928.

'You will remember that you asked me in Mussoorie about kings, and what they were, and why they became kings. We are now going to have a little peep in those far-off days when kings began....'

The Patriarch – how He Began

I am afraid my letters are getting a little complicated! But the life we see around us is itself very complicated. In the old days it was much simpler, but we are now considering the time when complications first began. If we follow up our inquiry slowly, and try to understand the changes in life and society as they came in, we shall find it easier to understand many things today. And if we do not try to do so, we shall never be able to understand all that is happening around us. We shall be like children lost in a dark forest. It is for this reason that I am trying to take you right back to the edge of the forest so that we may be able to find a way through it.

You will remember that you asked me in Mussoorie about kings, and what they were, and why they became kings. We are now going to have a little peep in those far-off days when kings began. They were not called kings to begin with. But if we try to find out something about them, we shall know the origin of kings.

I have told you already about the formation of tribes. When agriculture came, and there was some division of work or labour, it became necessary for some person in the tribe to organize the work. Even before this, the tribes wanted someone to lead them to battle against another tribe. The leader was usually the oldest man in the group. He was called or rather we call him now, the patriarch. As the oldest, he was supposed to be the most experienced and to have the most knowledge. This patriarch was not very different from the other members of the tribe. He worked with the others, and all the food that was produced was divided between all the members of the tribe. Everything belonged to the tribe. It was not like we have now, each person having his separate house and money and many other things. Whatever a man earned was divided up as it all belonged to the tribe. The patriarch or the organizer of the tribe did this dividing.

But changes came in slowly. There were new kinds of work, especially on account of agriculture, and the patriarch had to spend most of his time in organizing, and seeing that work was properly done by all the members of the tribe. Little by little, the patriarch gave up doing the ordinary work or labour of the people. He thus became quite different from the rest of the people. We see now another kind of division of work or labour: the patriarch doing the organizing and ordering people about, and the other people working in the fields and hunting and going to battle, and obeying the orders of their leader, the patriarch. If there was a war or a fight between two tribes, the patriarch became even more powerful, for in wartime it was not possible to fight well without a leader. So the patriarch became very powerful.

As the work of organizing increased, the patriarch could not do it all by himself. He chose other people to help him. So we have many organizers. But of course the patriarch was the chief. The tribe was then divided up into organizers and ordinary workers. Men were no longer more or less equal. Some men, who were the organizers, had power over the other men, who were the ordinary workers. We shall see how the patriarch developed in our next letter.

The Patriarch – how He Developed

I hope you do not find my account of the old tribes and their patriarchs very dull. I told you in my last letter that everything in those days belonged to the whole tribe and not to each member separately. Even the patriarch had nothing special to himself. As a member of the tribe, he could only have a share like any other member. But he was the organizer and he was supposed to look after the goods and property of the tribe. As his power increased, he began to think that these goods and property were really his own and not the tribe's. Or rather he thought that he himself, being the leader of the tribe, represented the tribe. So we see how the idea of owning things for oneself began. Today we are always thinking and talking of this thing being 'mine' or 'yours'. But, I have told you, the men and women of the first tribes did not think in this way. Everything then belonged to the tribe.

The old patriarch, however, began to think that he was the tribe, and so he looked upon most of the things belonging to the tribe as his own.

When the patriarch died, all the members of the tribe gathered together and chose another person to be their leader or patriarch. But usually the family of the patriarch knew more about the work of organization than the others. As they were always with the patriarch, they used to help him in his work and so they got to know about it. It so happened therefore that when an old patriarch died, the members of the tribe chose someone else from the same family.

So we find that the patriarch's family became different from the others and the tribe always chose its leaders from this family. Now the patriarch had a great deal of power. Naturally, he wanted his own son or brother to succeed him as patriarch and he tried his best to bring this about. So he trained his son or brother or some other near relative so that he might succeed him. He even told the tribe that a certain person whom he had selected and trained must become patriarch after him. Perhaps to begin with, the members of the tribe did not like being told so, but they soon got used to it and always did what the patriarch wanted them to do. There was practically no election or choosing of a new patriarch. The old man had already decided who was to be his successor and this man succeeded.

So we see that the office of the patriarch became hereditary, that is, it remained in the same family and went from father to son or some other relative. The patriarch now was quite sure that the property and things belonging to the tribe were really his own. Even when he died they remained in his family. We see how the idea of anything belonging to 'me' or 'you' started. There was no such idea to begin with. People all worked together for the tribe and not for themselves. If they produced a lot of food or other things, everybody in the tribe got his share. There were no rich or poor in the tribe. They were all sharers in the property of the tribe.

But as soon as the patriarch started grabbing at the things belonging to the tribe and calling them his own, we begin to get rich people and poor people.

I shall have something more to say about this in my next letter.

The Patriarch Becomes the King

The old patriarch has taken up a lot of our time, has he not? We shall finish with him soon, or rather he will change his name. I started by promising to tell you how kings came and what they were. And in order to understand kings one has to go right back to the patriarchs. You must have guessed that these patriarchs became later on kings or raja and maharaja. The word patriarch comes from the Latin 'Pater' or father. He was the leader and father of his tribe or people. 'Patria', which means fatherland or one's own country, comes from the same Latin word. You know that in French it is 'Patrie'. In Sanskrit and Hindi, we think of our country as the mother or motherland – *Matribhumi*, the motherland. Which do you prefer?

When the patriarch's office became hereditary, that is son succeeded father, there was little difference between him and a king. He developed into a king and the king got the strange notion that everything in the country belonged to him. He thought he was the country. A famous French king once said *L'état, c'est moi* – 'The State, it is I' or 'I am the State'. Kings forgot that they were really chosen by the people in order to organize and distribute the food and other things of the country among the people. They forgot that they were chosen because they were supposed to be the cleverest and the most experienced persons in the tribe or country. They imagined that they were the masters and all the other people in the country their servants. As a matter of fact, they were the servants of the country.

Later on, you will see when you read history that kings became so conceited that they thought that the people had nothing to do with choosing them. It was God himself, they said, that had made them kings. They called this the 'divine right of kings'. For long years, they misbehaved like this and lived in great pomp and luxury while their people starved. But, at last, the common people could not bear it any longer and in some countries they drove out their kings. You will read all about this later, how the people of England rose againtst their King Charles I and defeated him and even put him to death; how the people of France had a great revolution and decided to have no more kings. You will remember that we visited the Conciergerie prison in Paris. Were you with us then? In this prison were kept the members of the king's family, his wife Marie Antoinette and others. You will also read about the great Russian revolution when the people of Russia, only a few years ago, drove out their king, who was called the Tsar.

So kings have had their day and most countries have no kings. France and Germany and Russia and Switzerland and the countries of America and China and many other countries have no kings. They are republics, that is, the common people choose their governors and leaders from time to time. These governors and leaders are not hereditary.

In England, as you know, there is still a king, but he has no power. He can do very little. All the power belongs to the Parliament, where the chosen leaders of the people sit. You will remember seeing the Parliament in London.

In India, we have still many rajas and maharajas and nawabs. You see them going about with fine clothes, in expensive motor cars and spending a lot of money on themselves. Where do they get all this money from? They get it in taxes from the people. The taxes are given so that the money may be used to help all the people in the country – by making schools and hospitals and libraries and museums and good roads and many other things for the good of the people. But our rajas and maharajas still think as the French king did of old: *L'état c'est moi* – The State, it is I. And they spend the money of the people on their own pleasures. While they live in luxury, their people, who work hard and give them the money, starve and their children have no schools to go to.

JAYANT VISHNU NARLIKAR

EXTRACT FROM *THE SCIENTIFIC EDGE: THE INDIAN SCIENTIST FROM VEDIC TO MODERN TIMES.*

'The Delhi Observatory in a way commemorates the reestablishment, with Jai Singh's support, of order if not leadership in Delhi after years of anarchy following Aurangzeb.'

Indian Astronomy: Colonial Collaborations

The era from Aryabhata to Bhaskara II . . . belongs to the so-called period of Siddhantic astronomy. The word *Siddhanta* means *that whose end is established*, and it implies that the stress during this period was on the mathematical aspects of astronomy. Most likely this development owed its origin to the Greek influence on India following Alexander's invasion. Thus the use of algebra, geometry and trigonometry for calculation of planetary orbits and prediction of planetary position at a specified time were the high points of the texts written during the Siddhantic period.

Although Bhaskara II (born AD* 1114) was the last of the greats in this period, there were others who continued the tradition after him, such as Parameshwara (1380–1460) of Kerala. The interaction with the Arabs grew towards the end

* *Now commonly referred to as CE.*

of the first millennium AD, and the Arabic sources frequently refer to one Kanak al-Hindi who played a major role in promoting this interaction. (The Indian sources, however, do not mention anyone of that name!) His involvement seems to be in the preparation of *Zij al-Sindhind* (the Arabic translation of *Brahma-sphuta-siddhanta* by Brahmagupta). Other books that were written at this time were *Karanas*, which sought to simplify and provide practical examples of the formulae proved in the *Siddhantas*.

Let's now consider an important aspect of the period following that of the Siddhantic astronomy. This phase of post-Siddhantic world astronomy actually lacks a suitable name. Arab astronomy is a misnomer because most of the astronomers in this period were non-Arabs. Islamic astronomy is politically incorrect, and in the Indian context factually incorrect as well because contrary to general belief this astronomy was Sanskritized. The more recent term, Central and West Asian astronomy, is rather laboured and spatially restrictive. We may use the term Zij astronomy for this phase, because the main occupation of its astronomers was the preparation of Zijes (astronomical table). Zijes fall into three categories: Zij-e-Rashadi (direct tables) based on actual observations, Zij-e-Hisabi (calculated tables) obtained by correcting observational tables for errors, precession, etc; and Zij-e-Tas'hil (simplified tables), which were simplified versions of other tables, for example, tables for the moon alone. The Zij period began in the ninth century in Baghdad with the translation of Brahmagupta's Sanskrit works into Arabic, and it essentially came to an end in India with the compilation of *Zij-e-Muhammad Shahi* in 1728 by Raja Jai Singh Sawai.

Jai Singh and the Zij Astronomy

Zij astronomy made its debut in India under the patronage of King Firuz Shah Tughluq, who ruled in Delhi from 1351 to 1388. Arabic and Persian Zijes were copied and commented upon. Several books on astronomy were written during his reign and astrolabes (instruments for measuring the altitude of a star) were constructed. On his orders, an astrolabe was placed on Ferozabad, the highest minar of his capital in Delhi. Abul Fazl (1551–1602) the historian during the reign of Akbar, the Mogul emperor, listed in his *Ain-e-Akbari* eighty-six Zijes, from Zij-e-Hipparchus (first century BC*) to Zij-e-Gurgani (fifteenth century). Abu Mulla Farid Dehalvi, writing in the reign of Emperor Shah Jahan (1627–59), classified all the Zijes compiled to date. Owen Gingerich, research professor of astronomy and history of science at the Harvard-Smithsonian Center for Astrophysics, has pointed out that there were at Lahore four generations of astrolabe makers whose instrument design remained virtually unchanged for a century and a half. This suggests that these instruments were meant for drawing-room decoration rather than actual observations. Some of them in any case were too big and heavy for actual use.

In addition, Firuz Shah also took steps to Sanskritize instrumentation astronomy. On his orders, Mahendra Suri, head astronomer at the royal court, prepared in 1370 the *Yantra-raja*, a monograph on astrolabes. This was the first Sanskrit work exclusively devoted to instrumentation, and it was the subject of many later commentaries. In about

* *Now commonly referred to as BCE.*

1400, Padmanabha described an astrolabe made to a design different from Suri's and therefore taken from a different source. More importantly, he also described an instrument (*dhruva-bhramana-yantra*) that measures time by observation of the star group Polar Fish, which includes Alpha and Beta Ursae Minoris. Table 1* lists Sanskrit texts exclusively devoted to astronomical instruments. As one can seen from the tables, Siddhantic and Zij astronomies flourished side by side for a while.

Astronomical Instruments à la Jai Singh

From the eighteenth century, we have Raja Jai Singh Sawai's treatise on instruments, *Yantra-prakara*, essentially completed before 1724 but with some additions made up to 1729. His astronomer Jagannatha translated in 1732 Nasir al Din al Tusi's (1201–1274) Arabic recension of Ptolemy's *Almagest* into Sanskrit under the title *Samrata-siddhanta*, adding a supplement that described various instruments. Jai Singh went on to establish a number of pretelescopic masonry observatories. The Delhi Observatory, set up from 1721 to 1724, was followed by a bigger one at his new capital Jaipur (1728–1734). He built smaller ones at Mathura, Ujjain and Varanasi between 1723 and 1734. (These dates cannot be stated with greater precision for lack of historical detail.) The Varanasi Observatory was housed in an already existing building; it is probable that Jai Singh renovated an old observatory. Since Jai Singh's instruments and observations have been extensively dealt

* *On the following page.*

with in the literature, we shall therefore examine the political and scientific context of his work.

TABLE 1: Instrumentation Texts in Sanskrit

Year	Author (Place)	Work	Instrument
1370	Mahendra Suri (Delhi)	*Yantraraja*	astrolabe
c. 1400	Padmanabha	*Yantra-kiranvali*	astrolabe and *dhruva-bhramana-yantra*
1428	Ramachandra (Sitapur, UP)	*Yantra-prakasha*	miscellaneous
Fifteenth century	Hema (Gujarat)	*Kasha-yantra*	cylindrical sundial
b. 1507	Ganesha Daivajna	*Pratoda-yantra* *Sudhi-ranjana-yantra*	cylindrical sundial graduated strip
c. 1550–1650	Chakradhara (Godavari)	*Yantra-chintamani*	quadrant
1572	Bhudhara (Kampilya)	*Turiya-yantra-prakasha*	quadrant
c. 1580–1640	Jambusara Vishrama (Gujarat)	*Yantra-shiromani* (1615)	miscellaneous
c. 1720	Dadabhai Bhatta	*Turiya-yantropatti*	based on Chakradhara's work
1688–1743	Jai Singh Sawai (Jaipur)	*Yantra-prakara* *Yantraraja-rachana*	miscellaneous astrolabe
c. 1690–1750	Jagannatha (Jaipur)	*Samrata-siddhanta* (1732)	translation of *Almagest* with supplement on instruments

c. 1700–1760	Lakshmipati	*Dhruva-bhramana-yantra* *Samrata-yantra*	
c. 1700	Nayansukha Upadhyaya	*Yantraraja-risala-bisa-baba* or *Yantraraja-vichara vimshadhyay*	translation of manuscript on astrolabe by Nasir al Din al Tusi (thirteenth century, Iran)
c. 1750–1810	Nandarama Mishra (Kamyakavana, Rajasthan)	*Yantra-sara* (1772)	miscellaneous
c. 1750–1810	Mathuranatha Shukla (Varanasi)	*Yantraraja-ghatana* (1782)	astrolabe
c. 1736–1811	Chintamani Dikshit	*Golananda* (1800)	miscellaneous

Jai Singh was not a sovereign ruler. As an upper-level *mansabdar* (high-ranking official of the administration) who was paid for his services by allotment of land as *jagirs*, he owed allegiance to the Mogul emperor. He held his *vatan jagir* (hereditary dominion), which is retroactively called Jaipur. He also held various other *jagirs* that were granted to him by the emperor from time to time. He came to the throne of Amber in 1699. In 1702–03, when a mere lad of fourteen, he participated in Aurangzeb's war campaigns against the Marathas and acquitted himself well. His epithet *Sawai* (literally, one and a quarter) distinguishes him from his more illustrious ancestor of the same name, who is also called Mirza Raja. (The two Jai Singhs have often been confused.) Jai Singh came of age at a time when the once mighty Mogul Empire had started losing influence and power. His own rise in the court hierarchy was in direct proportion to the weakening of the central power. From 1712 to 1737 he served variously as the Governor of the provinces of Agra and Malwa. He was dismissed from both the posts in 1737. Jai Singh received huge funds from the emperor for enlisting troops against the Marathas, which he divided between the Marathas and himself, and preferred to spend his time at his capital. He had dreams of making his own peace with the Marathas and carving out a vast independent kingdom for himself. He failed in both the missions, but in 1727 he built a new capital, Jaipur, named after himself.

In its heyday, the Mogul Empire was responsible for creation of spectacular buildings (like the Taj Mahal) and gardens. In the reign of the later, lesser Moguls, the cultural activity in keeping with the general atmosphere of intrigue became *haveli* (mansion) oriented. The pastimes of nobility in this period were degeneracy, music and poetry. Jai Singh was an exception. Though not averse to intrigue, he was inspired by the earlier illustrious Moguls rather than his own contemporaries. He stands out as unique amongst Indian rulers in showing interest and support for science. It is significant that Jai Singh's observatories are the only visible astronomical effort in the whole of the Sultanate and Mogul periods.

Jai Singh's interest in astronomy was no doubt genuine. But astronomy was also his refuge, and probably a political statement, too. The year 1720 was one of rejoicing for Muhammad Shah because he had just freed himself from the clutches of the kingmakers in Delhi. A grand durbar was held on 25 November 1720 where Jai Singh successfully pleaded for the abolition of *jazia*, the hated tax on Hindus. It is probably at this durbar (or when Jai Singh attended the imperial court a few months later in July 1721) that Jai Singh took the royal permission for building his observatory. Incidentally, Jai Singh's astronomical role model, the martyr-prince Ulugh Beg of Samarkand, was also a collateral ancestor of the Mogul dynasty. The Delhi Observatory in a way commemorates the reestablishment, with Jai Singh's support, of order if not leadership in Delhi after years of anarchy following Aurangzeb. In a similar manner, Jaipur and its observatory symbolize Jai Singh's own imperial dreams. There is an element of irony in Jai Singh's nomenclature for his astronomical work *Zij-e-Muhammad Shahi* (completed 1728) is probably the only genuine tribute Raja Jai Singh ever paid to his ineffectual but charming emperor.

Jai Singh's Astronomical Tables

Even more ironically from a scientific point of view, the most remarkable feature of Jai Singh's astronomy is its anachronism. When he came on the scene, the telescope had been in use in Europe for more than 100 years, observatories had been set up in Paris and Greenwich, and many important discoveries made. The telescope was a revolutionary break with the past. It freed astronomy from the physical limitations of the eye and was therefore an instrument of the future. Brass and masonry instruments, on the other hand, had reached a dead end, even if they were no worse than the earliest telescopic instruments. Jai Singh failed to recognize the significance of European development. There was not an iota of doubt in Jai Singh's mind that he need not look beyond Samarkand for inspiration. To him European developments were either not impressive or were unreliable.

For example, in 1728 when Jai Singh's own observational tables were finally ready, he sponsored a scientific delegation to Portugal. Led by the Jesuit priest Father Emmanuel Figueredo, the delegation left in 1728 for Lisbon and returned a year and a half later in 1730 armed with mathematical books and some instruments, presumably telescopes. He tried the imported instruments and found them wanting. Most importantly, the delegation brought back Philippe de la Hire's (1640–1718) rather inconsequential *Tabulae Astronomicae*, which were prepared at the Paris Observatory and published in 1687 with a revised edition in 1702. These tables were enthusiastically received at Jaipur and promptly translated. Although most of the data in Jai Singh's tables are his own, he did borrow from La Hire technical details in refraction corrections, geographical coordinates of a number of places and probably the equation of time. Very soon it was discovered that La Hire's tables were not the last word. In many places, they did not match the observations. Using the terminology with which he was familiar, Jai Singh attributed these discrepancies to the 'inferior diameter' of La Hire's instruments. He invited Jesuit priests from the French factory (a fortified warehouse) at Chandernagore in Bengal for consultations. Father Claude Boudier (1686–1757) arrived at Jaipur in 1734 and confirmed that La Hire's tables were indeed defective. Jai Singh planned to send another delegation to Europe, but his death in 1743 put an end to his plans.

Jai Singh's choice of Portugal for scientific consultancy was ill-conceived. Its riches had come a long time ago, in the pre-Galilean era, and been spent in Mogul-style pomp and extravagance. Devoid of any scientific credentials whatsoever, Portugal was in no position to offer any enlightenment to Jai Singh because it was by then occupying a back seat in European science. The eighteenth century belonged to France and England, which were engaged in bitter commercial and naval rivalry. Both were great patrons of astronomy because of its utility as a valuable navigational aid. Moreover, astronomy became a fashion among the new rich in Europe. It might have been possible for Jai Singh to emulate the European rich and acquire from Paris or London some good quality instruments and use them visually. Or, using his position at the imperial court, he could have asked for and received astronomical instruments as gifts from any of the trading companies. European sailors and traders would have found it profitable to sell their astronomical instruments to Jai Singh and even educate him on their use, if he had so wished. It would certainly have been a rewarding experience because he would have had the southern skies to himself.

The scientific climate of eighteenth-century India stood in sharp contrast to the one in France and England. Europe needed modern astronomy and therefore developed technology for its sake. Traditional craftsmen were persuaded to make the much needed precision instruments in collaboration with the astronomers themselves. A turning point in history does not look for precedents. Jai Singh's India, on the other hand, had no use for astronomy, modern or medieval. Astronomy here was no more than a pastime and was therefore geared to the available technology. When Jai Singh could not get the desired brass instrument made, he tamely gave in and fell back on masonry, in keeping with the long Indian tradition of building imposing palaces, temples and mosques, although his instruments are less precise than Ulugh Beg's.

Jai Singh's edifice of science did not survive for long. In 1745, two years after Jai Singh's death, Emperor Muhammad Shah invited Father Andre Strobel to come to Delhi and take charge of the observatory. He declined. In 1764 the observatory was severely vandalized when Javahar Singh, son of Suraj Mal, the Jat Raja of Bharatpur, plundered Delhi. More than 150 years later, then the maharaja of Jaipur perfunctorily renovated the observatory to give it a presentable look at the time of the 1911 Delhi durbar of King George V. (The Delhi and Jaipur Observatories are now in a rather dilapidated state and no more than popular tourist spots.) Perhaps the most telling commentary on Jai Singh's dedicated but largely irrelevant scientific enterprise comes from the rather disconcerting fact that his grandson converted the Jaipur Observatory into a gun factory and used his ancestral 400-kilogram brass astrolabe (the *Samrat-yantra*) for target practice.

European Influence

While Jai Singh's observatories at Jaipur and Delhi today are local tourist attractions, at the Inter-University

Centre for Astronomy and Astrophysics (IUCAA) in Pune a copy of Jai Singh's *Samrat-yantra* constructed as per the latitude at Pune stands as a working testimony to Jai Singh's contributions to astronomy. The instrument is part of IUCAA'S science park for schoolchildren, where working scientific models explain the laws of science by providing hands-on experience to the user. The *Samrat-yantra* demonstrates how it can be used in daytime as a giant sundial, with the shadow of its inclined edge falling on its curved arc. A magnificent civil structure like this does not fail to impress the users, but it also tells them the story of a missed opportunity, which could have facilitated the entry of a good telescope into India in the eighteenth century.

In an earlier chapter, we contrasted the development of science in India and Europe, offering some explanation as to why the former waned as the latter began to blossom. As an example of the European stress on technology for use in solving life's problems, we may cite the invention of the telescope. In 1608–09 Hans Lippershey, a Dutch optician, accidentally discovered the telescope as he found his assistant gazing through two lenses at a pretty face across the street. Lippershey realized that by a suitable combination of lenses, the image of a distant object can be made larger and clearer. And so the telescope came into existence and found the military amongst its most avid users. It was certainly convenient and advantageous to be able to view the enemy's army formations and deployment from afar.

In 1609 Galileo Galilei learnt of this new invention and immediately saw its potential for observational astronomy.

Could not the distant heavenly bodies be brought closer and viewed more clearly with this instrument, just like the distant armies? Being practical-minded, Galileo made a few modifications to the original design in order to make the first astronomical telescope. With the main lens hardly one inch in diameter, it may look puny besides today's ten-metre Keck telescope, but its impact on astronomy was revolutionary.

JIM CORBETT

Extract from *My India.*

'Next second there was a terrifying roar as the tiger came crashing through the brushwood towards us... standing on its hind legs it clasped the tree, pinning Har Singh against it...'

Kunwar Singh

Kunwar Singh was by caste a Thakur, and the headman of Chandni Chauk Village. Whether he was a good or a bad headman I do not know. What endeared him to me was the fact that he was the best and the most successful poacher in Kaladhungi, and a devoted admirer of my eldest brother Tom, my boyhood's hero.

Kunwar Singh had many tales to tell of Tom, for he had accompanied him on many of his *shikar* expeditions, and the tale I like best, and that never lost anything in repetition, concerned an impromptu competition between brother Tom and a man by the name of Ellis, whom Tom had beaten by one point the previous year to win the B.P.R.A. gold medal for the best rifle-shot in India.

Tom and Ellis, unknown to each other, were shooting in the same jungle near Garuppu, and early one morning, when the mist was just rising above the treetops, they met on the approach to some high ground overlooking a wide depression in which, at that hour of the morning, deer and pig were always to be found. Tom was accompanied by

Kunwar Singh, while Ellis was accompanied by a *shikari* from Nainital named Budhoo, whom Kunwar Singh despised because of his low caste and his ignorance of all matters connected with the jungles. After the usual greeting, Ellis said that, though Tom had beaten him by one miserable point on the rifle range, he would show Tom that he was a better game shot; and he suggested that they should each fire two shots to prove the point. Lots were drawn and Ellis, winning, decided to fire first. A careful approach was then made to the low ground, Ellis carrying the 450 Martini-Henry rifle with which he had competed at the B.P.R.A. meeting, while Tom carried a 400 D.B. express by Westley-Richards of which he was justly proud, for few of these weapons had up to that date arrived in India.

The wind may have been wrong, or the approach careless. Anyway, when the competitors topped the high ground, no animals were in sight on the low ground. On the near side of the low ground there was a strip of dry grass beyond which the grass had been burnt, and it was on this burnt ground, now turning green with sprouting new shoots, that animals were to be seen both morning and evening. Kunwar Singh was of the opinion that some animals might be lurking in the strip of dry grass, and at his suggestion he and Budhoo set fire to it.

When the grass was well alight and the drongos, rollers, and starlings were collecting from the four corners of the heavens to feed on the swarms of grasshoppers that were taking flight to escape from the flames, a movement was observed at the farther edge of the grass, and presently two big boars came out and went streaking across the burnt ground for the shelter of the tree jungle three hundred yards away. Very deliberately Ellis, who weighed fourteen stone, knelt down, raised his rifle and sent a bullet after the hindmost pig, kicking up the dust between its hind legs. Lowering his rifle, Ellis adjusted the back sight to two hundred yards, ejected the spent cartridge, and rammed a fresh one into the breach. His second bullet sent up a cloud of dust immediately in front of the leading pig.

This second bullet deflected the pigs to the right, bringing them broadside on to the guns, and making them increase their speed. It was now Tom's turn to shoot, in a hurry, for the pigs were fast approaching the tree jungle, and getting out of range. Standing four-square, Tom raised his rifle and, as the two shots rang out the pigs, both shot through the head, went over like rabbits. Kunwar Singh's recital of this event invariable ended up with: 'And then I turned to Budhoo, that city-bred son of a low-caste man, the smell of whose oiled hair offended me, and said, "Did you see that, you, who boasted that your sahib would teach mine how to shoot? Had my sahib wanted to blacken the face of yours he would not have used two bullets, but would have killed both pigs with one".' Just how this feat could have been accomplished, Kunwar Singh never told me, and I never asked, for my faith in my hero was so great that I never for one moment doubted that, if he had wished, he could have killed both pigs with one bullet.

Kunwar Singh was the first to visit me that day of days when I was given my first gun. He came early, and as with great pride I put the old double-barrelled muzzle-loader into his hands he never, even by the flicker of an eyelid, showed that he had seen the gaping split in the right barrel, or the lappings of brass wire that held the stock and the barrels together. Only the good qualities of the left barrel were commented on, and extolled; its length, thickness, and the years of service it would give. And then, laying the gun aside, he turned to me and gladdened my eight-year-old heart and made me doubly proud of my possession by saying: 'You are now no longer a boy, but a man; and with this good gun you can go anywhere you like in our jungles and never be afraid, provided you learn how to climb trees; and I will now tell you a story to show how necessary it is for us men who shoot in the jungles to know how to do so.

'Har Singh and I went out to shoot one day last April, and all would have been well if a fox had not crossed our path as we were leaving the village. Har Singh, as you know, is a poor *shikari* with little knowledge of the jungle folk, and when, after seeing the fox, I suggested we should turn round and go home he laughed at me and said it was child's talk to say that a fox would bring us bad luck. So we continued on our way. We had started when the stars were paling, and near Garuppu I fired at a *chital* stag and unaccountably missed it. Later Har Singh broke the wing of a peafowl, but though we chased the wounded bird as hard as we could it got away in the long grass, where we lost it. Thereafter, though we combed the jungles we saw nothing to shoot, and towards the evening we turned our faces towards home.

'Having fired two shots, and being afraid that the forest guards would be looking for us, we avoided the road and took a sandy *nullah* that ran through dense scrub and thorn-bamboo jungle. As we went along talking of our bad luck, suddenly a tiger came out into the *nullah* and stood looking at us. For a long minute the tiger stared and then it turned and went back the way it had come.

'After waiting a suitable time we continued on our way, when the tiger again came out into the *nullah*; and this time, as it stood and looked at us, it was growling and twitching its tail. We again stood quite still, and after a time the tiger quietened down and left the *nullah*. A little later a number of junglefowl rose cackling out of the dense scrub, evidently disturbed by the tiger, and one of them came and sat on a *haldu* tree right in front of us. As the bird alighted on a branch in full view of us, Har Singh said he would shoot it and so avoid going home empty-handed. He added that the shot would frighten away the tiger, and before I could stop him he fired.

'Next second there was a terrifying roar as the tiger came crashing through the brushwood towards us. At this spot there were some *runi* trees growing on the edge of the *nullah*, and I dashed towards one while Har Singh dashed towards another. My tree was nearer to the tiger, but before it arrived I had climbed out of reach. Har Singh had not learnt to climb trees when a boy, as I had, and he was still standing on the ground, reaching up and trying to grasp a branch, when the tiger, after leaving me, sprang at him. The tiger did not bite or scratch Har Singh, but standing on its hind legs it clasped the tree, pinning Har Singh against it, and then started to claw big bits of bark and wood off the far side of the tree. While it was so engaged, Har Singh was screaming and the tiger was roaring. I had taken my gun up into the tree with me, so now, holding on with my bare feet, I cocked the hammer and fired the gun off into the air. On hearing the shot so close to it the tiger bounded away, and Har Singh collapsed at the foot of the tree.

'When the tiger had been gone some time, I climbed down very silently, and went to Har Singh. I found that one of the tiger's claws had entered his stomach and torn the lining from near his navel to within a few fingers' breadth of the backbone, and that all his insides had fallen out. Here was great trouble for me. I could not run away and leave Har Singh, and not having any experience in these matters, I did not know whether it would be best to try and put all that mass of insides back into Har Singh's stomach, or cut it off. I talked in whispers on this matter with Har Singh, for we were afraid that if the tiger heard us it would return and kill us, and Har Singh was of the opinion that his insides should be put back into his stomach. So, while he lay on his back on the ground, I stuffed it all back, including the dry leaves and grass and bits of sticks that were sticking to it. I then wound my pugree round him, knotting it tight to keep everything from falling out again, and we set out on the seven-mile walk to our village, myself in front, carrying the two guns, while Har Singh walked behind.

'We had to go slowly, for Har Singh was holding the pugree in position, and on the way night came on and Har Singh said he thought it would be better to go to the hospital at Kaladhungi than to our village; so I hid the guns, and we went the extra three miles to the hospital. The hospital was closed when we arrived, but the doctor babu who lives near by was awake, and when he heard our story he sent me to call Aladia the tobacco seller, who is also postmaster at Kaladhungi and who receives five rupees pay per month from the Government, while he lit a lantern and went to the hospital hut with Har Singh. When I returned with Aladia, the doctor had laid Har Singh on a string bed and, while Aladia held the lantern and I held the two pieces of flesh together, the doctor sewed up the hole in Har Singh's stomach. Thereafter the doctor, who is a very kind man of raw years and who refused to take the two rupees I offered him, gave Har Singh a drink of very good medicine to make him forget the pain in his stomach and we went home and found our womenfolk crying, for they thought we had been killed in the jungle by dacoits, or by wild animals. So you see, Sahib, how necessary it is for us men who shoot in the jungles to know how to climb trees, for if Har Singh had had someone to advise him when he was a boy, he would not have brought all that trouble on us.'[1]

I learnt many things from Kunwar Singh during the first few years that I carried the old muzzle-loader, one of them being the making of mental maps. The jungles we hunted in, sometimes together, but more often alone – for Kunwar Singh had a horror of dacoits and there were times when for weeks on end he would not leave his village – were many hundreds of miles square with only one road running through them. Times without number when returning from a shoot I called in at Kunwar Singh's village, which was three miles nearer the forest than my house was, to tell him I had shot a *chital* or *sambhar* stag, or maybe a big pig, and to ask him to retrieve the bag. He never once failed to do so, no matter in how great a wilderness of tree or scrub or grass jungle I had carefully hidden the animal I had shot, to protect it from vultures. We had a name for every outstanding tree, and for every water hole, game track and *nullah*. All our distances were measured by the imaginary flight of a bullet fired from a muzzle-loader, and all our direction fixed by the four points of the compass. When I had hidden an animal, or Kunwar Singh had seen vultures collected on a tree and suspected that a leopard or a tiger had made a kill, either he or I would set out with absolute confidence that we would find the spot indicated, no matter what time of day or night it might be.

After I left school and started work in Bengal I was only able to visit Kaladhungi for about three weeks each year, and I was greatly distressed to find on one of these annual visits that my old friend Kunwar Singh had fallen a victim to the curse of our foothills, opium. With a constitution weakened by malaria, the pernicious habit grew on him, and though he made me many promises he had not the moral strength to keep them. I was therefore not surprised, on my visit to Kaladhungi one February, to be told by the men in our village that Kunwar Singh was very seriously ill. News of my arrival spread through Kaladhungi that night, and next day Kunwar Singh's youngest son, a lad of eighteen, came hot-foot to tell me that his father was at death's door, and that he wished to see me before he died.

As headman of Chandni Chauk, paying the Government land revenue of four thousand rupees, Kunwar Singh was an important person, and lived in a big stone-built house with a slate roof in which I had often enjoyed his hospitality. Now as I approached the village in company with his son, I heard the wailing of women coming, not from the house, but from a small one-roomed hut Kunwar Singh had built for one of his servants. As the son led me towards this hut, he said his father had been moved to it because the grandchildren disturbed his sleep. Seeing us coming, Kunwar Singh's eldest son stepped out of the hut and informed me that his father was unconscious, and that he only had a few minutes to live.

I stopped at the door of the hut, and when my eyes had got accustomed to the dim light, made dimmer by a thick pall of smoke which filled the room, I saw Kunwar Singh lying on the bare mud floor, naked, and partly covered with a sheet. His nerveless right arm was supported by an old man sitting on the floor near him, and his fingers were being held round the tail of a cow (This custom of a dying man being made to hold the tail of a cow – preferably that of a black heifer – has its origin in the Hindu belief that when the spirit leaves its earthly body it is confronted with a river of blood, on the far side of which sits the Judge before whom the spirit must appear to answer for its sins. The heifer's tail is the only way by which the departing spirit can cross the river, and if the spirit is not provided with means of transit it is condemned to remain on earth, to be a torment to those who failed to enable it to appear before the judgment seat). Near Kunwar Singh's head was a brazier with cow-dung cakes burning on it, and by the brazier a priest was sitting, intoning prayers and ringing a bell. Every available inch of floor space was packed with men, and with women who were wailing and repeating over and over again, 'He has gone! He has gone!'

I knew men died like this in India every day, but I was not going to let my friend be one of them. In fact, if I could help it he would not die at all, and anyway not at present. Striding into the room I picked up the iron brazier, which was hotter than I expected it to be, and burnt my hands.

This I carried to the door and flung outside. Returning, I cut the bark rope by which the cow was tethered to a peg driven into the mud floor, and led it outside. As these acts, which I had performed in silence, became evident to the people assembled in the room, the hubbub began to die down, and it ceased altogether when I took the priest's arm and conducted him from the room. Then, standing at the door, I ordered everyone to go outside; the order was obeyed without a murmur or a single protest. The number of people, both old and young, who emerged from the hut was incredible. When the last of them had crossed the doorstep, I told Kunwar Singh's eldest son to warm two seers of fresh milk and to bring it to me with as little delay as possible. The man looked at me in blank surprise, but when I repeated the order he hurried off to execute it.

I now re-entered the hut, pulled forward a string bed which had been pushed against the wall, picked Kunwar Singh up and laid him on it. Fresh air, and plenty of it, was urgently needed, and as I looked round I saw a small window which had been boarded up. It did not take long to tear down the boards and let a stream of clean sweet air blow directly from the jungles into the overheated room which reeked with the smell of human beings, cow dung, burnt ghee, and acrid smoke.

When I picked up Kunwar Singh's wasted frame, I knew there was a little life in it, but only a very little. His eyes, which were sunk deep into his head, were closed, his lips were blue, and his breath was coming in short gasps. Soon, however, the fresh, clean air began to revive him and his breathing became less laboured and more regular, and presently, as I sat on his bed and watched through the door the commotion that was taking place among the mourners whom I had ejected from the death chamber, I became aware that he had opened his eyes and was looking at me; and without turning my head, I began to speak.

'Times have changed, uncle, and you with them. There was a day when no man would have dared to remove you from your own house, and lay you on the ground in a servant's hut to die like an outcaste and a beggar. You would not listen to my words of warning and now the accursed drug has brought you to this. Had I delayed but a few minutes in answering your summons this day, you know you would by now have been on your way to the burning ghat. As headman of Chandni Chauk and the best *shikari* in Kaladhungi, all men respected you. But now you have lost that respect, and you who were strong, and who ate of the best, are weak and empty of stomach, for as we came your son told me nothing has passed your lips for sixteen days. But you are not going to die, old friend, as they told you you were. You will live for many more years, and though we may never shoot together again in the Garuppu jungles, you will not want for game, for I will share all I shoot with you, as I have always done.

'And now, here in this hut, with the sacred thread round your fingers and a pipal leaf in your hands, you must swear an oath on your eldest son's head that never again will you touch the foul drug. And this time you will, and you *shall* keep your oath. And now, while we wait for the milk your son is bringing, we will smoke.'

Kunwar Singh had not taken his eyes off me while I was speaking, and now for the first time he opened his lips and said, 'How can a man who is dying smoke?'

'On the subject of dying,' I said, 'we will say no more, for as I have just told you, you are not going to die. And as to how we will smoke, I will show you.'

Then, taking two cigarettes from my case, I lit one and placed it between his lips. Slowly he took a pull at it, coughed, and with a very feeble hand removed the cigarette. But when the fit of coughing was over, he replaced it between his lips and continued to draw on it. Before we had finished our smoke, Kunwar Singh's son returned carrying a big brass vessel, which he would have dropped at the door if I had not hurriedly relieved him of it. His surprise was understandable, for the father whom he had last seen lying on the ground dying, was now lying on the bed, his head resting on my hat, smoking. There was nothing in the hut to drink from, so I sent the son back to the house for a cup; and when he had brought it I gave Kunwar Singh a drink of warm milk.

I stayed in the hut till into the night, and when I left Kunwar Singh had drunk a seer of milk and was sleeping peacefully on a warm and comfortable bed. Before I left I warned the son that he was on no account to allow anyone to come near the hut; that he was to sit by his father and give him a drink of milk every time he awoke; and that if on my return in the morning I found Kunwar Singh dead, I would burn down the village.

The sun was just rising next morning when I returned to Chandni Chauk to find both Kunwar Singh and his son fast asleep and the brass vessel empty.

Kunwar Singh kept his oath, and though he never regained sufficient strength to accompany me on my *shikar* expeditions, he visited me often and died peacefully four years later in his own house and on his own bed.

LEILA SETH

EXTRACT FROM *ON BALANCE: AN AUTOBIOGRAPHY.*

'Eight-year-old Tuttu ... pushed some money into her hands... Ever since Daddy's death he had been saving up his pocket money and it was all of two rupees.'

Memories of Father and a Home

When I was ten years old I got minor chorea. In Darjeeling, nobody had heard about this malady, so it took a long time before it was diagnosed. I gradually lost control of the left side of my body. My left hand and foot would not respond to my instructions. If I was carrying a cup, I would suddenly drop it. If I was trying to tie a knot, my left-hand fingers would stall and I would have to pull the string with my teeth. When walking, my left foot would go awry. My mother thought I was being disobedient and careless, and scolded me. But when she discovered I was ill, she smothered me with care and affection. The disease was also known as Saint Vitus's dance, because the affected limbs went on a frolic of their own.

My parents took me out of school in Darjeeling for the year, and I stayed with them in Calcutta. My mother tried to get me into school in Loreto House, Calcutta, but without success. So I studied at home with a teacher. The good thing about this unexpected move was that I got an opportunity to spend time with my father and to get to know him. Thank God for that. Little did I realize that a year later he would be dead.

My father was lot of fun and tried to cheer me up. He had given me a statue of the three monkeys: see no evil; hear no evil; speak no evil. It is one of my very special possessions. He referred to me as his little monkey, part of his Bandar Log. In fact, he made up a poem for me, which I later pasted into my autograph book:

Pyare, Pyare, Bandar Log,
Rahte Ghar Ke Andar Log,
Mewa, Mithai Lagate Bhog,
Tum Ho Pure Bandar Log.

With lots of love to Leila Bandarwa

(Dear little monkeys,
Always staying at home;
Nuts and goodies are your treat.
You are perfect little monkeys.)

But he also treated me like an adult and we would discuss many things. He taught me Pelmanism as a way to improve my memory. We went for early morning walks together – just the two of us – in the Horticultural Gardens near the Belvedere Railway Colony where we lived. He told me about positive thinking and what an effect it had in overcoming illness. He complained that whenever he criticized Ma, she burst into tears rather than meeting the criticism with discussion, and he advised me, if I didn't agree with something, to try and persuade the other person with logical arguments. Tears were not the answer, he felt; in fact, they irritated him.

My father had a very bad temper and would lose it easily. But he would quickly forget what he had said and later be surprised that the other person nursed a grudge. He had a lovely sense of humour and when he was home, the house was full of jokes and laughter. He was very fair and handsome and had twinkling brown eyes; in fact, he looked like an Englishman until he spoke. His thin crop of hair was soft and slightly silvered. But he was not very tall – about five feet five inches. Ma, by contrast, was tall for an Indian woman; she was five feet four inches, had fairly broad shoulders and was big-boned. She was round-faced like her name, the moon, had large black eyes and an aquiline nose and was altogether lovely. On the right side of her chin she had three black moles, arranged like the mathematical abbreviation for 'therefore', which set off her face. My parents were a good-looking couple.

Daddy loved books and taught me to love them, too. But he always wanted us to read two books at any given time – one of fiction or light reading and the other something serious. He said reading light novels one after the other was like eating too many sweets, which was bad for the teeth and the stomach. A balanced diet was necessary, so that you not only enjoyed yourself but also learnt something. He often repeated the phrase, 'Books are one's best friends and are the lifeblood of a master spirit.'

Daddy used to work very hard and was always short of time. But he wanted to give us something of himself. He taught us our multiplication tables and we had to repeat them to him while he shaved in the morning. He would suddenly interrupt us and ask, 'What is 3 x 16?' and we would have to reply promptly to gain his praise.

Despite his Hindu upbringing, he did not believe in observing rituals or doing puja daily – but he taught us the Gayatri Mantra and told us to recite OM instead of counting sheep when we couldn't sleep. We also celebrated our festivals with gusto, especially Holi and Diwali.

We were taught that a smiling face was a beautiful face. Each morning we were with Daddy a mirror was passed around and we had to look into it and smile and see the difference. Having worked on our beauty, we were then given a spoonful of honey with four almonds that had been soaked overnight and peeled, to enhance our digestion and intelligence.

One day, while Daddy was at the office, a man came to our house with a great many glittering gifts and even some toys. My eyes were shining just looking at them. But my mother refused to take anything and told him to go away. He was very unhappy, and requested her not to insult him and at least accept a token gift of a pair of blue *papier-mâché* vases, painted with a design of flowers and peacocks. As they were clearly not very expensive, my mother agreed to keep them. I wondered what the man had meant about feeling insulted.

When my father came home in the evening, all hell broke loose. He was furious with my mother for having kept even those two vases. According to my father, the man had some business dealings with the railway and what he had given amounted to a bribe, however small. My mother and I could not understand how such a paltry gift could be interpreted as a bribe. But my father said that, whereas on a grey or black sheet many marks might go unobserved, on a white sheet even a speck of grey would show. He reminded my mother of the one and only time he had allowed her to take her young sister with them in the railway saloon-car without a ticket, and there had been a check.

Much later, in the seventies, I shifted to Delhi. I used to drive myself to the Supreme Court and High Court and around the city. One day I saw the old Tilak Marg Railway Bridge being knocked down. I was attached to the bridge, as I had heard that my father was the superintendent engineer when it was built, and felt sad that it was to go. But when the workmen complained about the difficulty they were having in bringing down the bridge because it was so strong, bonded together with pure cement and tough to destroy, I felt extremely proud. It seemed to me to symbolize my father's reputation.

When my father was Senior Government Inspector of Railways, we often spent out holidays touring with him in his white saloon-car. The saloon was a little home in itself and consisted of a drawing-cum-dining room, two bedrooms, a bathroom, a toilet and a kitchenette. It would be connected to a train and then disconnected at a station where Daddy had to work. Since we were not allowed to cook while the train was moving, for fear of fire, my mother carried a lot of tinned food, fruit and biscuits to keep us happy and well-fed. It was like a perpetual picnic. We sang songs loudly and tunelessly, played Monopoly with great enthusiasm, and engaged in Blind Man's Buff and pillow fights. There was no refrigerator in the saloon in those days and we had to make do with an icebox in which the butter and cheese were preserved. Drinking water was carried in *surhais* and we had a special wooden stand with a handle for ours, so that the *surhai* didn't wobble and topple over. It would be refilled at the station from a tap marked 'Hindu Water'. There was no air-conditioner either, but trays with slabs of ice would be brought into the compartment and the fan put on 'full', to make the place delightfully cool.

After my father died, we suddenly had to travel in Inter class or third class as we could not afford to travel first or second. This was quite a come-down for us who had always travelled by train in a saloon or at least on a first-class pass. My mother was very unhappy at this sudden change. She was used to travelling in style and now there were only hard wooden berths, and our co-passengers were not of the same class as us. She wept bitterly the first time she had to take us in a third-class, overcrowded compartment, with people spitting and shouting all around us. She tried to keep her brood together and clean up the area we were all squashed in. It was truly hard for her. Daddy had told us never to use the toilet when the train was standing at a station, as it created problems of hygiene. So when we saw other passengers going to the toilet when the train was stationary, we tried to stop them – but they laughed at us in scorn.

When Daddy died, Ma was about thirty-six years old. Michi bhai was sixteen, Sashi bhai was thirteen and Tuttu was only eight. I was just shy of twelve. Ma was not qualified to earn any money. The Imperial Railway Service for which Daddy had worked was not a pensionable service at that time so there was only a small provident fund. Even after his own marriage, Daddy had spent money for the wedding of his younger sister Kalyani and educated his youngest brother, Shanti, in Germany to become a dentist. So there were no real savings and it was difficult for my mother to know how to manage things. At first she thought she would go and live with Babujee in his large house on Jopling Road in Lucknow.

That winter in Lucknow, I was very ill. It was diagnosed as the infectious and deadly diphtheria. My mother was desperately upset; she had just lost her husband, and she was now faced with the loss of her daughter. Babujee was distraught: his colleagues had told him that there was no medicine available in India for this illness. A film had started forming across my throat, and it was difficult and painful for me even to swallow my own spittle. Once the membrane covered the entire opening, it would be the end.

Babujee made inquiries about how to get the medicine from England. One of the doctors who came to see me told him that he had recently treated a young girl for diphtheria. Her parents had managed, with great difficulty and at great expense, to get the medicine from England, but the girl had died before it arrived. The family might still have the medicine in their refrigerator. But it was hard to know how to approach them in their present sorrow. In the event, the doctor did speak to them; they willingly gave him the medicine and would not accept any payment, saying: 'We couldn't save our daughter, but we would be happy if the medicine saves someone else's.'

Babujee loved us, but was very strict. Bhabhijee was kind, but didn't show her emotions. Sadly, things did not work out well between her and my mother owing to misunderstandings created by Ma's sister-in-law. But where could Ma go? We had no home and hardly any money or income. She wrote to the Dutts about her problems in Lucknow. They immediately invited her to come and live with them in their home in Darjeeling.

Michi bhai had finished school at St. Paul's, Darjeeling. He was now invited by the school to come and teach there for a term. Mr Goddard (called 'Pa' by the boys), who was the Rector of the school, realized my mother's financial predicament; this was his way of helping out. My elder brothers were very good students and had been an asset to the school. My younger brother Tuttu, though only eight, was showing signs of promise. St. Paul's was a boarding school and the fees were high, so Ma was thinking of withdrawing Sashi bhai and Tuttu and putting them in a day school, though she was loath to do so. But even if she did, where would they live? How could four of us live with the Dutts? It was an unbearable burden to impose on them in terms of both space and money.

While my mother was desperately wondering what to do, she suddenly received a letter from the Rector informing her that a substantial scholarship would be available for the education of Sashi and Tuttu, and expressing the hope that she would decide to keep them in school till they finished their studies. This was a huge relief, and we therefore returned to Darjeeling – the boys to St. Paul's and mother and I to stay with the Dutts. We were full of gratitude to them for their affection and their offer of protection.

***

When Daddy died after a prolonged illness, I was in Darjeeling with the Dutts. As usual I was staying with them when my mother was away. Aunty Dutt was very fond of my father, who called her Sergeant-Major, because she was tough and a strict disciplinarian. She called him Engineer Sahib.

My mother was with my father in the Railway Hospital in Calcutta when he died. The news of his death must have come through to Darjeeling late at night. Aunty Dutt called me into her bedroom early in the morning. I thought that she was going to scold me for some wrongdoing, otherwise I would not have been summoned so early, even before going to school. When I went into her room, she was still lying in bed. She quietly asked me to sit down beside her. I thought that what I had done must be serious and she was going to slap me, but she held my hands very tenderly and told me that my father had died the night before and I had to be very brave and look after my mother. The news came as a complete shock, as I knew my father had been ill for a long time, but I had not expected him to die. I didn't know what I was supposed to do and how I could help my mother.

Aunty added that if I didn't want to go to school that day, I could stay at home. But Sanjoy was going to St. Joseph's School as usual and, not knowing what to do with myself at home the whole day, I also decided to go. The nuns were very sympathetic; they commiserated with me at the untimely death of my father – 'He was such a young man,' they said. But to me at eleven, forty-seven seemed a very long way off, and I retorted, 'No, no, he was not young, he was an old man, he was forty-seven.' Now, of course, at seventy-three, I think I am young and feel that old age is at least ten years away. If I live to be eighty-three, I wonder what I will think then.

My father died on the night of 27 September 1942 and I became twelve about three weeks later on 20 October. It was a very special birthday as I was reaching the age of reason, and my mother had earlier written to me that she would come to Darjeeling and we would celebrate it in a big way. I was quietly excited about this and had been making many plans. But, of course, when my father died she didn't come to Darjeeling for a while. Her father managed to come to Calcutta with great difficulty; almost all the train services were disrupted owing to the Quit India agitation started against the British on 9 August 1942.

Babjuee took Ma to Lucknow, and everyone thought that we would all live with him there. I didn't know what was happening and had not seen Ma or spoken to her since Daddy's death. I felt very cut off as the post was late in coming, owing to the dislocation of the trains. Making a trunk call was a big thing in those days and very rarely done. I missed Ma bitterly. Aunty Dutt was especially good to me and had a green woollen dress made for my birthday. She also prepared some of my favourite dishes, but told me that I couldn't ask friends over, as it was a time of mourning and not of celebration. So it was a very quiet and lonely birthday; truly the age of reason had arrived and it was a clear and cold dawn. There were no friends, no gifts, no warmth. But Aunty was wise; she presented me with Louisa May Alcott's *Little Women*, and I became totally absorbed in it.

My mother came to Darjeeling at the end of November to take us to Lucknow for the winter holidays and to decide on the future course of our lives. I got a real shock when I saw her. It was only then that the true import of my father's death hit me. She was dressed all in white – the widows' colour. The large maroonish-red powder bindi that used to adorn and light up her face was gone. Her beautiful coloured glass bangles had been broken; one gold bangle was all she wore on each wrist. No jewellery, no bright clothes, no smile – what remained was just a strained and courageous visage tense with grief and with worrying about how she would look after and properly educate the four of us. My heart went out to her but I didn't know what to say or do. Eight-year-old Tuttu however, pushed some money into her hands, telling her that she would need it now that Daddy was not there to provide for us. Ever since Daddy's death he had been saving up his pocket money and it was all of two rupees.

MOHANDAS KARAMCHAND GANDHI

EXTRACT FROM *THE STORY OF MY EXPERIMENTS WITH TRUTH.*

'I was convicted of lying! That deeply pained me. How was I to prove my innocence?'

Childhood

I must have been about seven when my father left Porbandar for Rajkot to become a member of the Rajasthanik Court. There I was put into a primary school, and I can well recollect those days, including the names and other particulars of the teachers who taught me. As at Porbandar, so here, there is hardly anything to note about my studies. I could only have been a mediocre student. From this school I went to the suburban school and thence to the high school, having already reached my twelfth year. I do not remember having ever told a lie, during this short period, either to my teachers or to my schoolmates. I used to be very shy and avoided all company. My books and my lessons were my sole companions. To be at school at the stroke of the hour and to run back home as soon as the school closed – that was my daily habit. I literally ran back, because I could not bear to talk to anybody. I was even afraid lest anyone should poke fun at me.

There is an incident which occurred at the examination during my first year at the high school and which is worth recording. Mr Giles, the Educational Inspector, had come on a visit of inspection. He had set us five words to write as a spelling exercise. One of the words was 'Kettle'. I had misspelt it. The teacher tried to prompt me with the point of his boot, but I would not be prompted. It was beyond me to see that he wanted me to copy the spelling from my neighbour's slate, for I had thought that the teacher was there to supervise us against copying. The result was that all the boys, except myself, were found to have spelt every word correctly. Only I had been stupid. The teacher tried later to bring this stupidity home to me, but without effect. I never could learn the art of 'copying'.

Yet the incident did not in the least diminish my respect for my teacher. I was by nature blind to the faults of elders. Later I came to know of many other failings of this teacher, but my regard for him remained the same. For I had learnt to carry out the orders of elders, not to scan their actions.

Two other incidents belonging to the same period have always clung to my memory. As a rule I had a distaste for any reading beyond my school books. The daily lessons had to be done, because I disliked being taken to task by my teacher as much as I disliked deceiving him. Therefore I would do the lessons, but often without my mind in them. Thus when even the lessons could not be done properly, there was of course no question of any extra reading. But somehow my eyes fell on a book purchased by my father. It was *Shravana Pitribhakti Nataka* (a play about Shravana's devotion to his parents). I read it with intense interest. There came to our place about the same time itinerant showmen. One of the pictures I was shown was of Shravana carrying, by means of slings fitted for his shoulders, his blind parents on a pilgrimage. The book and the picture left an indelible impression on my mind. 'Here is an example for you to copy,' I said to myself. The agonized lament of the parents over Shravana's death is still fresh in my memory. The melting tune moved me deeply, and I played it on a concertina which my father had purchased for me.

There was a similar incident connected with another play. Just about this time, I had secured my father's permission to see a play performed by a certain dramatic company. This play – *Harishchandra* – captured my heart. I could never be tired of seeing it. But how often should I be permitted to go? It haunted me and I must have acted *Harishchandra* to myself times without number. 'Why should not all be truthful like Harishchandra?' was the question I asked myself day and night. To follow truth and to go through all the ordeals Harishchandra went through was the one ideal it inspired in me. I literally believed in the story of Harishchandra. The thought of it all often made me weep. My common sense tells me today that Harishchandra could not have been a historical character. Still, both Harishchandra and Shravana are living realities for me, and I am sure I should be moved as before if I were to read those plays again today.

At the High School

I have already said that I was learning at the high school when I was married. We three brothers were learning at the same school. The eldest brother was in a much higher class, and the brother who was married at the same time as I was, only one class ahead of me. Marriage resulted in both of us wasting a year. Indeed the result was even worse for my brother, for he gave up studies altogether. Heaven knows how many youths are in the same plight as he. Only in our present Hindu society do studies and marriage go thus hand in hand.

My studies were continued. I was not regarded as a dunce at the high school. I always enjoyed the affection of my teachers. Certificates of progress and character used to be sent to the parents every year. I never had a bad certificate. In fact I even won prizes after I passed out of the second standard. In the fifth and sixth I obtained scholarships and rupees four and ten respectively, an achievement for which I have to thank good luck more than my merit. For the scholarships were not open to all, but reserved for the best boys amongst those coming from the Sorath Division of Kathiawad. And in those days there could not have been many boys from Sorath in a class of forty to fifty.

My own recollection is that I had not any high regard for my ability. I used to be astonished whenever I won prizes and scholarships. But I very jealously guarded my character. The least little blemish drew tears from my eyes. When I merited, or seemed to the teacher to merit, a rebuke, it was unbearable for me. I remember having once received corporal punishment. I did not so much mind the punishment, as the fact that it was considered my desert. I wept piteously. That was when I was in the first or second standard. There was another such incident during the time when I was in the seventh standard. Dorabji Edulji Gimi was the headmaster then. He was popular among boys, as he was a disciplinarian, a man of method and a good teacher.

He had made gymnastics and cricket compulsory for boys of the upper standards. I disliked both. I never took part in any exercise, cricket or football, before they were made compulsory. My shyness was one of the reasons for this aloofness, which I now see was wrong. I then had the false notion that gymnastics had nothing to do with education. Today I know that physical training should have as much place in the curriculum as mental training.

I may mention, however, that I was none the worse for abstaining from exercise. That was because I had read in books about the benefits of long walks in the open air, and having liked the advice, I had formed a habit of taking walks, which has still remained with me. These walks gave me a fairly hardy constitution.

The reason of my dislike for gymnastics was my keen desire to serve as nurse to my father. As soon as the school closed, I would hurry home and begin serving him. Compulsory exercise came directly in the way of this service. I requested Mr Gimi to exempt me from gymnastics so that I might be free to serve my father. But he would not listen to me. Now it so happened that one Saturday, when we had school in the morning, I had to go from home to the school for gymnastics at four o'clock in the afternoon. I had no watch, and the clouds deceived me. Before I reached the school the boys had all left. The next day Mr Gimi, examining the roll, found me marked absent. Being asked the reason for absence, I told him what had happened. He refused to believe me and ordered me to pay a fine of one or two annas (I cannot now recall how much).

I was convicted of lying! That deeply pained me. How was I to prove my innocence? There was no way. I cried in deep anguish. I saw that a man of truth must also be a man of care. This was the first and last instance of my carelessness in school. I have a faint recollection that I finally succeeded in getting the fine remitted. The exemption from exercise was of course obtained, as my father wrote himself to the headmaster saying that he wanted me at home after school.

But though I was none the worse for having neglected exercise, I am still paying the penalty of another neglect. I do not know whence I got the notion that good handwriting was not a necessary part of education, but I retained it until I went to England. When later, especially in South Africa, I saw the beautiful handwriting of lawyers and young men born and educated in South Africa, I was ashamed of myself and repented of my neglect. I saw that bad handwriting should be regarded as a sign of an imperfect education. I tried later to improve mine, but it was too late. I could never repair the neglect of my youth. Let every young man and woman be warned by my example, and understand that good handwriting is a necessary part of education. I am now of the opinion that children should first be taught the art of drawing before learning how to write. Let the child learn his letters by observation as he does different objects, such as flowers, birds, etc., and let him learn handwriting only after he has learnt to draw objects. He will then write a beautifully formed hand.

Two more reminiscences of my school days are worth recording. I had lost one year because of my marriage, and the teacher wanted me to make good the loss by skipping a class, a privilege usually allowed to industrious boys. I therefore had only six months in the third standard and was promoted to the fourth after the examinations which were followed by the summer vacation. English became the medium of instruction in most subjects from the fourth standard. I found myself completely at sea. Geometry was a new subject in which I was not particularly strong, and the English medium made it still more difficult for me. The teacher taught the subject very well, but I could not follow him. Often I would lose heart and think of going back to the third standard, feeling that the packing of two years' studies into a single year was too ambitious. But this would discredit not only me, but also the teacher; because, counting on my industry, he had recommended my promotion. So the fear of the double discredit kept me at my post. When, however, with much effort I reached the thirteenth proposition of Euclid, the utter simplicity of the subject was suddenly revealed to me. A subject which only required a pure and simple use of one's reasoning powers could not be difficult. Ever since that time geometry has been both easy and interesting for me.

Sanskrit, however, proved a harder task. In geometry there was nothing to memorize, whereas in Sanskrit, I thought, everything had to be learnt by heart. This subject also was commenced from the fourth standard. As soon as I entered the sixth I became disheartened. The teacher was a hard taskmaster, anxious, as I thought, to force the boys. There was a sort of rivalry going on between the Sanskrit and the Persian teachers. The Persian teacher was lenient. The boys used to talk among themselves that Persian was very easy and the Persian teacher very good and considerate to the students. The 'easiness' tempted me and one day I sat in the Persian class. The Sanskrit teacher was grieved. He called me to his side and said:

'How can you forget that you are the son of a Vaishnava father? Won't you learn the language of your own religion? If you have any difficulty, why not come to me? I want to teach you students Sanskrit to the best of my ability. As you proceed further, you will find in it things of absorbing interest. You should not lose heart. Come and sit again in the Sanskrit class.'

This kindness put me to shame. I could not disregard my teacher's affection. Today I cannot but think with gratitude of Krishnashankar Pandya. For if I had not acquired the little Sanskrit that I had learnt then, I should have found it difficult to take any interest in our sacred books. In fact I deeply regret that I was not able to acquire a more thorough knowledge of the language, because I have since realized that every Hindu boy and girl should possess sound Sanskrit learning.

It is now my opinion that in all Indian curricula of higher education there should be a place for Hindi, Sanskrit, Persian, Arabic and English, besides of course the vernacular. This big list need not frighten anyone. If our education were more systematic, and the boys free from the burden of having to learn their subjects through a foreign medium, I am sure learning all these languages would not be an irksome task, but a perfect pleasure. A scientific knowledge of one language makes a knowledge of other languages comparatively easy.

In reality, Hindi, Gujarati and Sanskrit may be regarded as one language, and Persian and Arabic also as one. Though Persian belongs to the Aryan, and Arabic to the Semitic family of languages, there is a close relationship between Persian and Arabic, because both claim their full growth through the rise of Islam. Urdu I have not regarded as a distinct language, because it has adopted the Hindi grammar and its vocabulary is mainly Persian and Arabic, and he who would learn good Urdu must learn Persian and Arabic, as one who would learn good Gujarati, Hindi, Bengali or Marathi must learn Sanskrit.

NANDAN NILEKANI

EXTRACT FROM *IMAGINING INDIA: IDEAS FOR THE NEW CENTURY.*

'The British had dived in and built their schools in India with the hope of creating a class of British-educated Indians who would enact and translate their agenda for the rest of the Indian population.'

S Is for Schools
The Challenges in India's Classrooms

By the time I meet the economist Dr Jeffrey Sachs in Delhi, he has been in India for a few weeks, and is somewhat sunburned, his cheeks a bright apple-red. I find him inimitably cheerful and enthusiastic about his trip – he has been touring villages across Uttar Pradesh, studying the progress of the government's new school education initiative. But when I ask him about his impression from visiting the village schools, his answer is cautious. 'There is a lot of change,' he says, 'but I wonder if there is enough of it. India has a lot of ground to cover on education, and very little time.'

I am familiar with this tone of wary optimism – I have caught it often in the remarks of NGO workers and the bureaucrats working with India's schools. Despite some signs of progress, our dilemmas in school education are very real; they are the small print that accompanies India's rise as a knowledge economy. We have some pretty shocking statistics when it comes to education: India produces the second largest number of engineers in the world every year, as well as the largest number of school dropouts. Even as India is building a name for itself in intellectual capital, a third of its population remains illiterate. Across cities, some of the best-equipped schools – with swimming pools and air-conditioned tennis courts – and the worst, lacking even a blackboard, exist across the street from one another. It is our schools that now delineate our class lines most prominently – even as middle-class parents compete to get their kids into the privately run Delhi Public School in RK Puram, parents in the RK Puram slums can do little more than place their children in the single-room slum school, or in the crumbling, dismal government school round the corner and hope for the best.

If this is our Achilles heel, it is significant enough to make the whole of us fragile. Few things are as wide-ranging in their impact on the economy as education. The collapse of our schools is a deep crack in India's foundation, and it impacts everything from our health achievements and fertility rates to our economic mobility and political choices. The evidence of our education failures is brought home to us every day – in the children selling magazines on city intersections, students dropping out from failing schools and accompanying their fathers to work, and companies facing shortages in educated workers in a billion-peopled country.

The crisis of our education system is not a new problem. Schooling in India has been a struggle, both before and since independence. But what has now changed is the growing awareness about education and a demand for it that cuts across income groups. 'The poor used to talk about education in a very vague sense ten years ago,' one literacy worker told me. 'They saw it as something that was "good" to do. Being educated was like being pious – it added to your character. But now there is a real sense of what people lose in incomes and opportunities from not attending school.' And this shift is driving some remarkable changes in our education policy.

The British-educated Indian

John Milton's *Paradise Lost* was only one among numerous British literary works that referred to the 'Orient' as a culturally infernal place – the East and India for the British was a region of 'barbaric despotism'.[1] By the nineteenth century, running down Indian culture was a popular intellectual exercise; British writers like John Stuart Mill described India as depraved, immoral, wild and populated by lost souls.

Our moral and cultural problems could only be addressed, in British eyes, by transmitting their culture to the country – through education and English schools. India was depicted as a 'sad, sleeping beauty' that needed new life: the kiss of British education. Charles Grant, making his pitch for British-style schools, called the Hindus malevolent and evil, adding that 'the true cure for darkness is light . . . the Hindoos err, because they are ignorant and their errors have never been laid before them.'[2]

The writings of these English administrators and historians greatly influenced Thomas Macaulay, the chairman of the General Committee of Public Instruction in India in the 1830s. With typical modesty, Macaulay asserted that Indians had 'no books on any subject which deserve to be compared to our own'. Thanks in part to the tirade that was his Minute on Education, the British resolution to bring English education to India was passed in 1835. But while this gave a new stress on British education, there was little initiative towards a *universal* system. Three universities were established by 1857, and approximately fifty English schools took root. Beyond that, growth was slow.

One reason for this apathy was that the very idea of universal education was far-fetched among the British. England did not have universal schooling – it was a privilege for the sons of squires, for the nobles and the rich. It was the last country in Europe to adopt compulsory education, and passed the law only in 1881. In India the British also did not have the money for it – the tiny parliamentary grant allocated for education to the Indian colony was just enough to set up the first universities and schools.

The British had dived in and built their schools in India with the hope of creating a class of British-educated Indians who would enact and translate their agenda for the rest of the Indian population. But the educated Indians that came out of these universities saw themselves not as brokers for the British but as brokers for the Indians – one Indian leader remarked in 1898 that they were 'the brains and conscience of the country . . . spokesmen of the illiterate masses'. This class of educated leaders immediately saw the potential of British education in social emancipation. Indian education had often been exclusionary and limited to the 'twice born' across Indian gurukuls, and leaders such as Raja Ram Mohan Roy applauded the possibilities English education offered, in eliminating the social evils of sati, caste discrimination and dowry. The backward caste leader Jyotirao Phule similarly wrote of the potential of British schools to 'construct a new society' and end 'Brahmin domination' by offering a window to liberal ideas.

These Indian leaders took note of the sparse network of the British schools, and began to pitch for schooling that was more accessible and widespread. In 1911 the Congress party leader Gopal Krishna Gokhale presented his universal education bill before Delhi's Imperial Legislative Council. He made an impassioned plea to the Council members. In a delicate reference to the salt tax, he said, 'It's a smaller evil that my countrymen should eat less salt, if that money could be spent on education.' And Lala Lajpat Rai, well aware of the British obsession with security, noted that inspiring Indians with patriotic thoughts 'through education' would be more effective than deploying armed guards and erecting barricades. But the council did not bite.[3]

With no real solutions forthcoming from the government, Indian leaders began to try out alternative education systems.* In 1920 the Nagpur Congress Session passed a resolution towards building 'national' schools and colleges. These schools would offer education in a 'nai talim' form suggested by Gandhi, where schools focused on teaching real-life skills, 'through the medium of village handicrafts like spinning and carding'.[4] Calling the British system 'satanic', Gandhi toured the country to persuade students to drop out of

* *There were political compulsions here as well – many leaders in Congress (and especially Gandhi) opposed the 'indoctrination' that was going on in English schools, and the teaching of Latin and Greek; they wanted an alternative more oriented towards Indian education and culture.*

British schools and join this national system. The effort was, however, a rather spectacular failure, since these schools were not recognized by the government and the economic rewards of British style education were substantial.

Gandhi was relentless in his support for 'basic education' that would translate into practical use. The Wardha committee of basic education in 1938 again recommended village handicrafts for boys, while offering, rather unfairly, domestic science for girls. Fortunately – since such education would have been very limited indeed – these ideas did not prevail, and invited criticism from the National Planning Committee, as well as from other Congress leaders.[5] The writer Mulk Raj Anand wrote that such schools would only create 'morons that vegetate within the limits of their self-sufficient village communities'.[6]

Forgotten Ambitions

It was a tiny part of the nation that could read the headlines and the unfurled banners declaring India's independence in 1947. By that year, the disparities in education were huge abysses – they stretched between the rich and the poor, women and men, and the backward and the privileged castes. Literacy in the country was a low 12 per cent, and enrollment in schools averaged 40 per cent.

The limited access to schools meant that education in India became more or less an inherited trait. One study of IFS officers showed that nearly half of the recruits during 1947–56 and 1956–63 had had their fathers working in the civil service.[7] Most of the educated employees in both the public and the private sectors were graduates from a small, privileged circle of approximately fifty prominent government and public schools, and a select group of church- and convent-managed schools.

Indian leaders were acutely conscious of what these disparities meant. The first Education Commission in its 1954 report – which helped frame the national education policy – remarked that 'violent revolution' and chaos during India's economic development could be prevented by only one thing: education. But as the former member of the Planning Commission, L.C. Jain notes, 'The government had other concerns.' In the years leading up to independence, Jain was a student political leader, working undercover against the British Indian government. At the time of Partition, he helped manage the camps of refugees from Pakistan and house thousands of displaced people. This kind of experience was shared by many of the leaders in India's early governments, and it shaped their priorities – their focus was mainly on trying to unify a turbulent young nation, one already wounded by the creation of Pakistan and whose cities and towns were being periodically swallowed up in violence and riots. The stability required for successful education schemes was missing, and Partition had especially frayed the nerves of the country's first education minister, Maulana Azad. Azad as a result, Ramachandra Guha tells me, 'sat sulking in his tent', busy with relatively lightweight pet initiatives such as the Sangeet Natak Akademi and the Indian Council for Cultural Relations.

As Abhijit Banerjee* points out to me, if we consider the

* *Indian economist, currently the Ford Foundation International Professor of Economics at the Massachusetts Institute of Technology. (Not in original text.)*

early ambitious visions Indian leaders had, it was unusual for the government to not concentrate on education. 'Many visionary leaders, from as far back as Napoleon, have found the idea of building a nation through education a very attractive notion,' he says. But India's legislators did not really get that chance, thanks to the regional divides across the country that made a single, coherent education system impossible.* Delhi's focus on education and literacy got especially muddied when the states were allowed to teach in regional languages in their schools. And with education as a state subject, the centre's role in setting school standards and regulation became very limited.

Besides, budgets were terribly tight. 'The money allocated to education was just pitiful,' Jain says. 'Defence expenditure took a large bite out of the budget, over a hundred crore, while education had three or four crore.' He adds, 'The lack of money was a real tragedy. We had dynamic education secretaries who were just thirsting for resources.' The pint-sized amount allocated to schools worried ministers such as C. Subramaniam, and soon enough, with both money and a sense of urgency missing, education languished, kicked to the curb as India pursued other priorities of development.

Worse, education in India lacked a clear vision. Gandhi's ideas on school – that schooling for the masses needed to be practical, of the 'life skills' sort – had affected the views of many leaders. In this vein, Nehru suggested 'one-teacher schools' across India that would give 'basic, not

* *In fact, the Kothari Commission suggested a single system in the 1960s – a 'Common School System' across the country, a hot rod of a recommendation that no minister dared to touch.*

literary education . . . the education codes should not apply there'.

There was a real divide here between what the leaders said and the words of the Constitution. The dominant idea among India's early legislators was that the 'masses' did not require the full scale of school education, even though the Constitution had made a commitment in Article 45 that the state would provide within ten years, 'free and compulsory education for all children until they complete the age of fourteen'. In fact, in the assembly debates over the Constitution in 1948, the MP Lakshmi Kanta Maitra had demanded deleting the statement in Article 36 which said 'Every citizen is *entitled* to free primary education', since education, he argued, was not a fundamental right. Another member denounced the same constitutional article as 'pious hopes and pious wishes . . . meant to create trouble for the provincial Ministries'.[8]

This was in stark contrast with what India's neighbours were up to. In China, Mao pitched education as central to creating ' new men' motivated and fully literate in the party ideology. In East Asia, the Confucian ethic emphasized the need for education, and literacy was a necessary virtue for the deeply religious. In the island country of Sri Lanka, the Buddhists were a strong force in encouraging literacy and education.

The religious and ideological momentum for education in these countries was similar to what had happened in most of Europe, where Martin Luther's growing influence had coincided with the rise of the printing press. This enabled the mass production of texts, and the rise of the Bible as a hugely popular book printed in languages other than the inaccessible Latin. The trend was helped by the sentiment that, to be truly faithful, people had to read the scriptures. Such religious forces were an immense boost towards mass literacy, especially among the rural classes who would not otherwise have seen the point of being able to read and write.

In India, however, religious traditions almost demanded the opposite. Among Hindus, religious stories, songs and literature were sung and recited, and you could be, if you wished, an illiterate person of faith. Besides, the rural 'upper' castes considered the idea of 'lower' castes learning to read texts – especially religious texts – sacrilegious. This was especially pronounced in the north and east of the country, where the odious idea of literacy as a privilege for certain castes persisted well into the 1970s, and dropouts among backward caste students were especially high in schools. In West Bengal in the 1970s, for instance, four out of every five students enrolling in schools belonged to the upper castes, and in secondary schools the figure was 98 per cent.

The dynamics of caste within villages only made things more dismal. Illiterate rural labour was a class of people that the landlords could easily dominate, especially since these workers depended on their landlords to handle government officers and manage their paperwork. The landowners, obviously keen to maintain the status quo, protested with a straight face that effective schooling created unreasonable expectations among the backward castes for better jobs and empowerment.[9] The government remained indifferent to these inequities, despite ambitious statements on education – in part because the political support they derived in rural India during the 1950s and

1960s was primarily from these large landowners and *jotdars*. It was a collaboration towards apathy.

For the poor, educating their children also meant enormous trade-offs. The reality of poor students in government schools, especially in the villages, was of 'pupils in rags, unwashed, their hair red from sun and malnutrition, and made stiff and blond with dust'.[10] For a family coping with meagre shelter, hard to come by meals and regular movements from place to place due to temporary jobs, schooling was an issue fraught with too much sacrifice. Sendhil Mullainathan, the Harvard economist who has taken a close look at poverty in his work at the university, tells me, 'Few of us can comprehend the day-to-day tragedy that the poorest people face. You have a limited daily wage, and your choice lies between everyday, urgent needs versus spending money on school books and uniforms to send your child to school. That's not an easy call.'

Another factor that education officials regularly brought up while defending low enrolment rates in schools was the reluctance of parents to give up money that working children earned. In poorer families, it was expected that children would be earning members; the writer Suma Chitnis remarked how students in a Bombay municipal school were absent en masse 'each time the neighbouring factory had a peak of production'. Many unorganized industries in India – bangle and glassware, matchsticks, fireworks, garment factories – hired child workers, some a young as three, in droves.

The social scientist Myron Weiner pointed out that this compulsion of poor parents to send children to work was used as a rationale by governments to not enforce compulsory education in India. Trying to teach these children, according to many education officers, was like hammering on cold iron – with parents unwilling, there was not much they could achieve. Time and again, these arguments ignored the interest and rights of the child in favour of the parent – perhaps this was a depressing reflection of the fact that the child, after all, could not vote.

School policy also presented Indian governments with a rather difficult and nuanced challenge. 'Education' of real and tangible value requires a mix of factors, ranging from qualified, inspired teachers to up-to-date curriculum and effective testing. But the Indian government's education approach has been clumsy and unwieldy. Through the 1960s and 1970s, the focus of governments in school education was on building infrastructure, with little emphasis on teachers' training, educational achievements and performance measurement. As a result the total number of illiterates continued to grow, even as states haplessly built school after ineffective school – schools that were hollow promises, with little teaching taking place within the buildings. Our education policies, as the writer Amit Varma put it, 'have funded schools, not schooling'.[11]

RABINDRANATH TAGORE

EXTRACT FROM *PERSONALITY*.

'Of course, it would be foolish to underrate the advantages of the book. But at the same time we must admit that the book has its limitations and its dangers.'

My School

I believe, as I suggested before, that children have their subconscious mind more active than their conscious intelligence. A vast quantity of the most important of our lessons has been taught to us through this. Experiences of countless generations have been instilled into our nature by its agency, not only without causing us any fatigue, but giving us joy. This subconscious faculty of knowledge is completely one with our life. It is not like a lantern that can be lighted and trimmed from outside, but it is like the light that the glow-worm possesses by the exercise of its life-process.

Fortunately for me I was brought up in a family where literature, music and art had become instinctive. My brothers and cousins lived in the freedom of ideas, and most of them had natural artistic powers. Nourished in these surroundings, I began to think early and to dream and to put my thoughts into expression. In religion and social ideals our family was free from all convention, being ostracized by society owing to our secession from orthodox beliefs and customs. This made us fearless in our freedom of mind, and we tried experiments in all departments of life. This was the education I had in my early days, freedom and joy in the exercise of my mental and artistic faculties. And because this made my mind fully alive to grow in its natural environment of nutrition, therefore the grinding of the school system became so extremely intolerable to me.

I had only this experience of my early life to help me when I started my school. I felt sure that what was most necessary was the breadth of culture and no formal method of teaching. Fortunately for me, Satish Chandra Roy, a young student of great promise, who was getting ready for his B.A. degree, became attracted to my school and devoted his life to carry out my idea. He was barely nineteen, but he had a wonderful soul, living in a world of ideas, keenly responsive to all that was beautiful and great in the realm of nature and of human mind. He was a poet who would surely have taken his place among the immortals of world literature, if he had been spared to live, but he died when he was twenty, thus offering his service to our school only for the period of one short year. With him boys never felt that they were confined in the limit of a teaching class; they seemed to have their access to everywhere. They would go with him to the forest when in the spring the *sal* trees were in full blossom, and he would recite to them his favourite poems, frenzied with excitement. He used to read to them Shakespeare and even Browning – for he was a great lover of Browning – explaining to them in Bengali with his wonderful power of expression. He never had any feeling of distrust for the boys' capacity of understanding; he would talk and read to them about whatever was the subject in which he himself was interested. He knew that it was not at all necessary for the boys to understand literally and accurately, but that their minds should be roused, and in this he was always successful. He was not like other teachers, a mere vehicle of textbooks. He made his teaching personal; he himself was the source of it, and therefore it was made of life-stuff, easily assimilable by the living human nature. The real reason of his success was his intense interest in life, in ideas, in everything around him, in the boys who came in contact with him. He had his inspiration not through the medium of books, but through the direct communication of his sensitive mind with the world. The seasons had upon him the same effect as they had upon the plants. He seemed to feel in his blood the unseen messages of nature that are always travelling through space, floating in the air, shimmering in the sky, tingling in the roots of the grass under the earth. The literature that he studied had not the least smell of the library about it. He had the power to see ideas before him, as he could see his friends, with all the distinctness of form and subtlety of life.

Thus the boys of our school were fortunate enough to be able to receive their lessons from a living teacher and not from textbooks. Have not our books, like most of our necessaries, come between us and our world? We have got into the habit of covering the windows of our minds with their pages, and plasters of book phrases have stuck into our mental skin, making it impervious to all direct touches of truth. A whole world of bookish truths have formed themselves into a strong citadel with rings of walls in which we have taken shelter, secured from the communication of

God's creation. Of course, it would be foolish to underrate the advantages of the book. But at the same time we must admit that the book has its limitations and its dangers. At any rate during the early period of education children should come to their lesson of truths through natural processes directly through persons and things.

Being convinced of this, I have set all my resources to create an atmosphere of ideas in the ashram. Songs are composed, not specially made to order for juvenile minds. They are songs that a poet writes for his own pleasure. In fact, most of my *Gitanjali* songs were written here. These, when fresh in their first bloom, are sung to the boys, and they come in crowds to learn them. They sing them in their leisure hours, sitting in groups, under the open sky on moonlit nights, in the shadows of the impending rain in July. All my latter-day plays have been written here, and the boys have taken part in their performance. Lyrical dramas have been written for their season-festivals. They have ready access to the room where I read to the teachers any new things that I write in prose or in verse, whatever the subject may be. And this they utilize without the least pressure put upon them, feeling aggrieved when not invited. A few weeks before leaving India I read to them Browning's drama *Luria*, translating it into Bengali as I went on. It took me two evenings, but the second meeting was as full as the first one. Those who have witnessed these boys playing their parts in dramatic performances have been struck with their wonderful power as actors. It is because they are never directly trained in the histrionic art. They instinctively enter into the spirit of the plays in which they take part, though these plays are no mere schoolboy dramas. They require subtle understanding and sympathy. With all the anxiety and hypercritical sensitiveness of an author about the performance of his own play, I have never been disappointed in my boys, and I have rarely allowed teachers to interfere with the boys' own representation of the characters. Very often they themselves write plays or improvise them, and we are invited to their performance. They hold meetings of their literary clubs, and they have at least three illustrated magazines conducted by three sections of the school, the most interesting of them being that of the infant section. A number of our boys have shown remarkable powers in drawing and painting, developed not through the orthodox method of copying models, but by following their own bent and by the help of occasional visits from some artists to inspire the boys with their own work.

When I first started my school my boys had no evident love for music. The consequence was that at the beginning I did not employ a music teacher and did not force the boys to take music lessons. I merely created opportunities when those of us who had the gift could exercise their musical culture. It has the effect of unconsciously training the ears of the boys. And when gradually most of them showed a strong inclination and love for music I saw that they would be willing to subject themselves to formal teaching, and it was then that I secured a music teacher.

In our school the boys rise very early in the morning, sometimes before it is light. They attend to the drawing of water for their bath. They make up their beds. They do all those things that tend to cultivate the spirit of self-help.

I believe in the hour of meditation, and I set aside fifteen minutes in the morning and fifteen minutes in the evening for that purpose. I insist on this period of meditation, not, however, expecting the boys to be hypocrites and to make-believe they are meditating. But I do insist that they remain quiet, that they exert the power of self-control, even though instead of contemplating on God, they may be watching the squirrels running up the trees.

Any description of such a school is necessarily inadequate. For the most important element of it is the atmosphere, and the fact that it is not a school which is imposed upon the boys by autocratic authorities. I always try to impress upon their minds that it is their own world upon which their life ought fully and freely to react. In the school administration they have their place, and in the matter of punishment we mostly rely upon their own court of justice.

RUSKIN BOND

EXTRACT FROM *THE BEST OF RUSKIN BOND*.

'. . . the world at large judges you according to who you are, rather than what you have done.'

Life at My Own Pace

All my life I've been a walking person. To this day I have neither owned nor driven a car, bus, tractor, aeroplane, motor boat, scooter, truck, or steamroller. Forced to make a choice, I would drive a steamroller, because of its slow solid progress and unhurried finality.

In my early teens I did for a brief period ride a bicycle, until I rode into a bullock-cart and broke my arm; the accident only serving to underline my unsuitability for wheeled conveyance that is likely to take my feet off the ground. Although dreamy and absent-minded, I have never *walked* into a bullock-cart.

Perhaps there is something to be said for sun signs. Mine being Taurus, I have, like the bull, always stayed close to grass, have lived my life at my own leisurely pace only being stirred into furious activity when goaded beyond endurance. I have every sympathy for bulls and none for bullfighters.

I was born in the Kasauli military hospital in 1934, and was baptized in the little Anglican church which still stands in the station. My father had done his schooling at the Lawrence Royal Military School, at Sanawar, a few miles away, but he had gone into 'tea' and then teaching, and at the time I was born he was out of a job. In any case, the only hospital in Kasauli was the Pasteur Institute for the treatment of rabies, and as neither of my parents had been bitten by a mad dog, it was the army who took charge of my delivery.

But my earliest memories are not of Kasauli, for we left when I was two or three months old; they are of Jamnagar, a small State in coastal Kathiawar, where my father took a job as English tutor to several young princes and princesses. This was in the tradition of Forester and Ackerley, but my father did not have literary ambitions, although after his death I was to come across a notebook filled with love poems addressed to my mother, presumably written while they were courting.

This was where the walking really began, because Jamnagar was full of palaces and spacious lawns and gardens, and by the time I was three I was exploring much of this territory on my own with the result that I encountered my first cobra, who, instead of striking me dead as the best fictional cobras are supposed to do, allowed me to pass.

Living as he did so close to the ground, and sensitive to every footfall, the intelligent snake must have known instinctively that I presented no threat, that I was just a small human discovering the use of his legs. Envious of the snake's swift gliding movements, I went indoors and tried crawling about on my belly, but I wasn't much good at it. Legs were better.

Amongst my father's pupils in one of these small States were three beautiful princesses. One of them was about my age, but the other two were older, and they were the ones at whose feet I worshipped. I think I was four or five when I had this strong crush on two 'older' girls – eight and ten respectively. At first I wasn't sure that they were girls, because they always wore jackets and trousers and kept their hair quite short. But my father told me they were girls, and he never lied to me.

My father's schoolroom and our own living quarters were located in one of the older palaces, situated in the midst of a veritable jungle of a garden. Here I could roam to my heart's content, amongst marigolds and cosmos growing rampant in the long grass, an ayah or a bearer often being sent posthaste after me, to tell me to beware of snakes and scorpions.

One of the books read to me as a child was a work called *Little Henry and His Bearer*, in which little Henry converts his servant to Christianity. I'm afraid something rather different happened to me. My ayah, bless her soul, taught me to eat *paan* and other forbidden delights from the bazaar, while the bearer taught me to abuse in choice Hindustani – an attribute that has stood over the years.

Neither of my parents were overly religious, and religious tracts came my way far less frequently than they do now. (*Little Henry* was a gift from a distant aunt.) Nowadays everyone seems to feel I have a soul worth saving, whereas, when I was a boy, I was left severely alone by both preachers and adults. In fact, the only time I felt threatened by religion was a few years later, when, visiting the aunt I have mentioned, I happened to fall down her steps and sprain my ankle. She gave me a triumphant look and said, 'See what happens when you don't go to church!'

My father was a good man. He taught me to read and write long before I started going to school, although it's true to say that I first learned to read *upside-down.* This happened because I would sit on a stool in front of the three princesses, watching them read and write and so the view I had of their books was an upside-down view; I still read that way occasionally, when a book gets boring.

He gave me books like *Peter Pan* and *Alice in Wonderland* (which I lapped up), but he was a fanatical stamp collector, with dozens of albums, and corresponded and dealt regularly with Stanley Gibbons in London. After he died, the collections disappeared, otherwise I might well have been left a fortune in rare stamps!

My mother was at least twelve years younger and liked going out to parties and dances. She was quite happy to leave me in the care of the ayah and bearer. I had no objection to the arrangement. The servants indulged me; and so did my father, bringing me books, toys, comics, chocolates, and of course stamps, when he returned from visits to Bombay.*

Walking along the beach, collecting seashells, I got into the habit of staring hard at the ground, a habit which has stayed with me all my life. Apart from helping my thought-processes, it also results in my picking up odd objects – coins, keys, broken bangles, marbles, pens, bits of crockery, pretty stones, ladybirds, feathers, snail-shells. Occasionally, of course, this habit results in my walking some way past my destination (if I happen to have one), and why not? It simply means discovering a new and different destination,

* *Now Mumbai.*

sights and sounds that I might not have experienced had I ended my walk exactly where it was supposed to end. And I am not looking at the ground all the time. Sensitive like the snake to approaching footfalls, I look up from time to time to examine the faces of passers-by, just in case they have something they wish to say to me.

A bird singing in a bush or tree has my immediate attention so does any unfamiliar flower or plant, particularly if it grows in an unusual place such as a crack in a wall or rooftop, or in a yard full of junk where I once found a rose-bush blooming on the roof of an old Ford car.

There are other kinds of walks that I shall come to later but it wasn't until I came to Dehradun and my grandmother's house that I really found my feet as a walker.

In 1939, when World War II broke out, my father joined the RAF, and my mother and I went to stay with her mother in Dehradun, while my father found himself in a tent in the outskirts of Delhi.

It took two or three days by train from Jamnagar to Dehradun, but trains were not quite as crowded then as they are today (the population being much smaller), and provided no one got sick, a long train journey was something of an extended picnic, with halts at quaint little stations, railway-meals in abundance brought by waiters in smart uniforms, an ever-changing landscape, bridges over mighty rivers, forest, desert, farmland, everything sun-drenched, the air clear and unpolluted except when dust storms swept across the plains. Bottled drinks were a rarity then, the occasional lemonade or 'vimto' being the only aerated soft drinks, apart from soda-water. We made our own orange juice or lime juice, and took it with us.

By journey's end we were wilting and soot-covered, but Dehra's bracing winter climate brought us back to life.

Scarlet poinsettia leaves and trailing bougainvilleas adorned the garden walls, while in the compounds grew mangoes, lichis, papayas, guavas, and lemons large and small. It was a popular place for retiring Anglo-Indians, and my maternal grandfather, after retiring from the Railways, had built a neat, compact bungalow on the Old Survey Road. There it stands today, unchanged except in ownership. Dehra was a small, quiet, garden-town, only parts of which are still recognizable, forty years after I first saw it.

I remember waking in the train early in the morning, and looking out of the window at heavy forest, trees of every description but mostly *sal* and *shisham*; here and there a forest glade, or a stream of clear water – quite different from the muddied waters of the streams and rivers we'd crossed the previous day. As we passed over a largish river (the Song) we saw a herd of elephants bathing; and leaving the forests of the Siwalik hills, we entered the Doon valley where fields of rice and flowing mustard stretched away to the foothills.

Outside the station we climbed into a tonga, or pony-trap, and rolled creakingly along quiet roads until we reached my grandfather's house. Grandfather had died a couple of years previously, and Grandmother had lived alone, except for occasional visits from her married daughters and their families, and from the unmarried but wandering son Ken, who was to turn up from time to time, especially when his funds were low. Granny also had a tenant, Miss Kellner, who occupied a portion of the bungalow.

Miss Kellner had been crippled in a carriage accident in

Calcutta when she was a girl, and had been confined to a chair all her adult life. She had been left some money by her parents, and was able to afford an ayah and four stout palanquin-bearers, who carried her about when she wanted the chair moved and took her for outings in a real sedan chair or sometimes a rickshaw – she had both. Her hands were deformed and she could scarcely hold a pen, but she managed to play cards quite dexterously and taught me a number of card games, which I have forgotten now, as Miss Kellner was the only person with whom I *could* play cards: she allowed me to cheat. She took a fancy to me, and told Granny that I was the only one of her grandchildren with whom she could hold an intelligent conversation; Granny said that I was merely adept at flattery. It's true Miss Kellner's cook made marvellous meringues, coconut biscuits and curry puffs, and these would be used very successfully to lure me over to her side of the garden, where she was usually to be found sitting in the shade of an old mango tree, shuffling her deck of cards. Granny's cook made a good kofta curry, but he did not go in for the exotic trifles that Miss Kellner served up.

Granny employed a full-time gardener, a wizened old character named Dukhi (sad), and I don't remember that he ever laughed or smiled. I'm not sure what deep tragedy dwelt behind those dark eyes (he never spoke about himself, even when questioned) but he was tolerant of me, and talked to me about flowers and their characteristics.

There were rows and rows of sweet peas; beds full of phlox and sweet-smelling snapdragons; geraniums on the veranda steps, hollyhocks along the garden wall. . . Behind the house were the fruit trees, somewhat neglected since my grandfather's death, and it was here that I liked to wander in the afternoons for the old orchard was dark and private and full of possibilities. I made friends with an old jack-fruit tree, in whose trunk was a large hole in which I stored marbles, coins, catapults, and other treasures much as a crow stores the bright objects it picks during its peregrinations.

I have never been a great tree-climber, having a tendency to fall off the branches, but I liked climbing walls (and still do), and it was not long before I had climbed the wall behind the orchard to drop into unknown territory and explore the bazaars and bylanes of Dehra.

***

'Great, grey, formless India,' as Kipling had called it, was, until I was eight or nine, unknown territory for me, and I had heard only vaguely of the freedom movement and Nehru and Gandhi; but then, a child of today's India is just as vague about them. Most domiciled Europeans and Anglo-Indians were apolitical. That the rule of the Sahib was not exactly popular in the land was made plain to me on the few occasions I ventured far from the house. Shouts of 'Red Monkey!' or 'White Pig!' were hurled at me with some enthusiasm but without any physical follow-up. I had the sense, even then, to follow the old adage, 'Sticks and stones may break my bones, but words can never hurt me.'

It was a couple of years later, when I was eleven, just a year or two before independence, that two passing cyclists, young men, swept past and struck me over the head. I was stunned but not hurt. They rode away with cries of triumph – I suppose it was a rare achievement to have successfully assaulted someone whom they associated with the ruling race – but although I could hardly (at that age) be expected to view them with Gandhian love and tolerance, I did not allow the resentment to rankle. I know I did not mention the incident to anyone – not to my mother or grandmother, not even to Mr Ballantyne, the S.P., a family friend who dropped in at the house quite frequently. Perhaps it was personal pride that prevented me from doing so; or perhaps I had already learnt to accept the paradox that India could be as cruel as it could be kind.

With my habit, already formed, of taking long walks into familiar areas, I exposed myself more than did most Anglo-Indian boys of my age. Boys bigger than me rode bicycles; boys smaller than me stayed at home!

My parents' marriage had been on the verge of breaking up, and I was eight or nine when they finally separated. My mother was soon married again, to a Punjabi businessman, while I went to join my father in his air force hutment in Delhi. I would return to Dehra, not once but many times in the course of my life, for the town, even when it ceased to enchant, continued to exert a considerable influence on me, both as a writer and as a person; not a literary influence (for that came almost entirely from books) but as an area whose atmosphere was to become a part of my mind and sensuous nature.

I had a very close relationship with my father and was more than happy with him in Delhi, although he would be away almost every day, and sometimes, when he was hospitalized with malaria, he would be away almost every night too. When he was free he took me for long walks to the old tombs and monuments that dotted the wilderness that then surrounded New Delhi; or to the bookshops and cinemas of Connaught Place, the capital's smart shopping complex, then spacious and uncluttered. I shared his fondness for musicals, and wartime Delhi had a number of cinemas offering all the glitter of Hollywood.

I wasn't doing much reading then – I did not, in fact, become a great reader until after my father's death – but played gramophone records when I was alone in the house, or strolled about the quiet avenues of New Delhi, waiting for my father to return from his office. There was very little traffic in those days and the roads were comparatively safe.

I was lonely, shy and aloof, and when other children came my way I found it difficult to relate to them. Not that they came my way very often. My father hadn't the time or the inclination to socialize, and in the evenings he would sit down to his stamp collection while I helped to sort, categorize and mount his treasures.

I was quite happy with this life. During the day, when there was nothing else to do, I would make long lists of films or book or records; and although I have long since shed this hobby, it had the effect of turning me into an efficient cataloguer. When I became a writer, the world lost a librarian or archivist.

My father felt that this wasn't the right sort of life for a growing boy, and arranged for me to go to a boarding school in Simla.* As often happens, when the time approached for

* *Now Shimla.*

me to leave, I did make friends with some other boys who lived down the road.

Trenches had been dug all over New Delhi, in anticipation of Japanese air raids, and there were several along the length of the road on which we lived. These were ideal places for games of cops and robbers, and I was gradually drawn into them. The heat of midsummer, with temperatures well over 100 degrees Fahrenheit, did not keep us indoors for long, and in any case the trenches were cooler than the open road. I discovered that I was quite strong, too, in comparison with most boys of my age, and in the wrestling bouts that were often held in the trenches I invariable came out, quite literally, on top. At eight or nine I was a chubby boy; I hadn't learnt to use my fists (and never did), but I knew how to use my weight, and when I sat upon an opponent he usually remained sat upon until I decided to move.

I don't remember all their names, but there was a dark boy called Joseph, Goan I think, who was particularly nice to me, no matter how often I sat upon him. Our burgeoning friendship was cut short when my father and I set out for Simla. My father had two weeks' leave, and we would spend that time together before I was shut up in school. Ten years in a boarding school was to convince me that such places bring about an unnatural separation between children and parents that is good for neither body nor soul.

That fortnight with my father was the only happy spell in my life for some time to come. We walked up to the Hanuman Temple on Jakko Hill; took a rickshaw-ride to Sanjauli, while my father told me the story of Kipling's phantom-rickshaw, set on that very road; ate ice creams at Davico's restaurant (and as I write this, I learn that this famous restaurant has just been destroyed in a fire); browsed in bookshops and saw more films; made plans for the future. 'We will go to England after the war.'

He was, in fact, the only friend I had as a child, and after his death I was to be a lonely boy until I reached my late teens.

School seemed a stupid and heartless place after my father had gone away. The traditions even in prep school – such is ragging and caning, compulsory games and daily chapel attendance, prefects larger than life, and Honours Boards for everything from School Captaincy to choir membership – had apparently been borrowed from *Tom Brown's Schooldays*. It was all part of the process of turning us into 'leaders of men'. Well, my leadership qualities remained exactly at zero, and in time I was to discover the sad fact that the world at large judges you according to who you are, rather than what you have done.

My father had been transferred to Calcutta and wasn't keeping well. Malaria again. And the jaundice. But his last letter sounded quite cheerful. He'd been selling his valuable stamp collection, so as to have enough money for us to settle in England.

One day my class teacher sent for me.

'I want to talk to you, Bond,' he said. 'Let's go for a walk.'

I knew it wasn't going to be a walk I would enjoy; I knew instinctively that something was wrong.

As soon as my unfortunate teacher (no doubt cursing the Headmaster for giving him such an unpleasant task) started on the theme of 'God wanting your father in a higher and better place' – as though there could be any better place than Jakko Hill in midsummer! – I knew my father was dead, and burst into tears.

Later, the Headmaster sent for me and made me give him the pile of letters from my father that I had been keeping in my locker. He probably felt it was unmanly of me to cling to them.

'You might lose them,' he said. 'Why not keep them with me? At the end of term, before you go home, you can come and collect them.'

Reluctantly I gave him the letters. He told me he had heard from my mother and stepfather and that I would be going to them when school closed.

At the end of the year, the day before school closed, I went to the HM's office and asked him for my letters.

'What letters?' he said. His desk was piled with papers and correspondence, and he was irritated by the interruption.

'My father's letters,' I explained. 'You said you would keep them for me, sir.'

'Letters, letters. Are you sure you gave them to me ?' He was growing more irritated. 'You must be mistaken, Bond. What would I want from your father's letters?'

'I don't know, sir. You said I could collect them before going home.'

'Look, I don't remember your letters and I'm very busy just now. So run along. I'm sure you're mistaken, but if I find any personal letters of yours, I'll send them on to you.'

I don't suppose his forgetfulness was anything more than the muddled indifference that grows in many of those who have charge of countless small boys, but for the first time in my life, I knew what it was like to hate someone.

And I had discovered that words could hurt, too.

SAROJINI NAIDU

Speech after Mahatma Gandhi's Assassination, broadcast from Delhi Station, All India Radio, on February 1, 1948.

'Shall sacrifice be in vain? Shall his blood be shed for futile purposes of mourning?'

My Father, Do not Rest!

Like Christ of old on the third day he has risen again in answer to the cry of his people and the call of the world for the continuance of his guidance, his love, his service and inspiration. And while we all mourn, those who loved him, knew him personally, and those to whom his name was but a miracle and legend, though we are all full of tears and though we are full of sorrow on this third day when he has risen from his own ashes, I feel that sorrow is out of place and tears become a blasphemy. How can he die, who through his life and conduct and sacrifice, who through his love and courage and faith has taught the world that the spirit matters, not the flesh, that the spirit has the power greater than the powers of the combined armies of the earth, combined armies of the ages! He was small, frail, without money, without even the full complement of garments to cover his body, not owning even as much earth as might be held on the point of a needle, how was he so much stronger than the forces of violence, the might of empires and the grandeur of embattled forces in the world?

Why was it that this little man, this tiny man, this man with a child's body, this man so ascetic, living on the verge of starvation by choice so as to be more in harmony with the life of the poor, how was it that he exercised over the entire world, of those who revered him and those who hated him, such power as emperors could never wield?

It was because he did not care for applause; he did not care for censure. He only cared for the path of righteousness. He cared only for the ideals that he preached and practised. And in the midst of the most terrible disasters caused by violence and greed of men, when the abuse of the world was heaped up like dead leaves, dead flowers on battlefields, his faith never swerved in his ideal of non-violence. He believed that though the whole world slaughter itself and the whole world's blood be shed, still his non-violence would be the authentic foundation of the new civilization of the world and he believed that he who seeks his life shall lose it and he who loses his life shall find it.

His first fast in 1924 with which I was associated was for the cause of Hindu-Muslim unity. It had the sympathy of the entire nation. His last fast was also for the cause of Hindu-Muslim unity, but the whole nation was not with him in that fast. It had grown so divided, it had grown so bitter, it had grown so full of hate and suspicion, it had grown so untrue towards the tenets of the various creeds in this country that it was only a section of those who understood the Mahatma who realized the meaning of that fast. It was very evident that the nation was divided in its loyalty to him in that fast. . .

. . . But it does not matter. It is a personal grief, that is, loss day in and day out, year in and year out, for many of us who cannot forget, because for more than 30 years some of us have been so closely associated with him that our lives and his life were an integral part of one another. Some of us are indeed dead to the faith: some of us indeed have had vivisection performed on us by his death, because fibres of our being, because our muscles, veins and heart and blood were all intertwined with his life.

But, as I say, it would be the act of faithless deserters if we were to yield to despair. If we were indeed to believe that he is dead, if we were to believe that all is lost, because he has gone, of what avail would be our love and our faith? Of what avail would be our loyalty to him if we dare to believe that all is lost because his body is gone from our midst? Are we not there, his heirs, his spiritual descendants, the legatees of his great ideals, successors of his great work? Are we not there to implement that work and enhance it and enrich and make greater achievements by joint efforts than he could have made singly? Therefore, I say the time is over for private sorrow.

The time is over for beating of breasts and tearing of hair. The time is here and now when we stand up and say, 'We take up the challenge' to those who defied Mahatma Gandhi. We are his living symbols. We are his soldiers. We are the carriers of his banner before an embattled world. Our banner is truth. Our shield is non-violence. Our sword is a sword of the spirit that conquers without blood. Let the peoples of India rise up and wipe their tears, rise up and still their sobs, rise up and be full of hope and full of cheer. Let us borrow from him, why borrow, he has handed it to us, the radiance of his own personality, the glory of his own courage, the magnificent epic of his character. Shall we not follow in the footsteps of our master? Shall we not obey the mandates of our father?

Shall not we his soldiers carry his battle to triumph? Shall we not give to the world the completed message of Mahatma Gandhi? Though his voice will not speak again, have we not a million, million voices to bear his message to the world, not only to this world, to our contemporaries, but to the world generation after generation? Shall sacrifice be in vain? Shall his blood be shed for futile purposes of mourning? Or, shall we not use that blood as a *tilak* on our foreheads, the emblem of his legion of peace-loving soldiers to save the world? Here and now, here and now, I for one, before the world that listens to my quivering voice, pledge myself and you, as I pledged myself more than thirty years ago, to the service of the undying Mahatma.

What is death? My own father, dying, just before his death with the premonition of death on him, said: 'There is no birth. There is no death. There is only the soul seeking higher and higher stages of truth.' Mahatma Gandhi who lived for truth in this world has been translated, though by the hand of an assassin, to a higher stage of the truth which he sought. Shall we not take up his place? Shall not our united strength be strong enough to preach and practise his great message for the world? I am here one of the lowliest of his soldiers, but along with me I know are his beloved disciples like Jawaharlal Nehru, like his trusted followers and friends – Vallabhbhai Patel, Rajendra Babu, who was like St John in the bosom of Christ, and those others of his associates who at a moment's notice flew from all ends of India to make their last homage at his feet. Shall we not all take up his message and fulfil it? I used to wonder very often during his many fasts in which I was privileged to serve him, to solace him, to make him laugh, because he wanted the tonic laughter of his friends – I used to wonder, supposing he died in Sevagram, supposing he died in Noakhali, supposing he died in some far-off place, how should we reach him? It is therefore right and appropriate that he died in the city of kings, in the ancient site of the old Hindu empires, in the site on which was built the glory of the Moghuls, in this place that he made India's capital, wresting it from foreign hands, it is right that he died in Delhi; it is right that his cremation took place in the midst of the dead kings who are buried in Delhi, for he was the kingliest of all kings. And it is right also that he who was the apostle of peace should have been taken to the cremation ground with all the honours of a great warrior; far greater than all warriors who led armies to battle was this little man, the bravest, the most triumphant of all. Delhi is not only today historically the Delhi of seven kingdoms; it has become the centre and the sanctuary of the greatest revolutionary who emancipated his enslaved country from foreign bondage and gave to it its freedom and its flag. May the soul of my master, my leader, my father, rest not in peace, not in peace, but let his ashes be so dynamically alive that the charred ashes of the sandalwood, the powder of his bones be so charged with life and inspiration that the whole of India will after his death be revitalized into the reality of freedom.

My father, do not rest. Do not allow us to rest. Keep us to our pledge. Give us strength to fulfil our promise, your heirs, your descendants, your stewards, the guardians of your dreams, the fulfillers of India's destiny. You, whose life was so powerful, make it so powerful in your death, far from mortality you have passed mortality by a supreme martyrdom in the cause most dear to you.

SARVEPALLI RADHAKRISHNAN

ADDRESS AT A CONVOCATION CEREMONY.

'Character is that on which the destiny of a nation is built.'

Address at the Convocation Ceremony, Karnataka University

. . . The times ahead of us are of a very difficult character. The movements which took place in other countries during a span of centuries have all occurred here more or less simultaneously. What answer to the Renaissance, the Reformation, the Industrial Revolution or the political Revolution – all these things have been telescoped so to say in these few years in our country. We have won political independence. But it is not to be regarded as giving us complete freedom. There are ever so many other things which require to be fulfilled if this first step is to be regarded as a preparation for the liberation of this great land. If we wish to follow up political revolution by a social and economic one, our universities must send out batches of scientists, technicians, engineers, agriculturists, etc.

These are essential for changing the face of our country, the economic character of our society. But we should not believe that science and technology alone are enough. There are other countries, much advanced countries in the world, which have achieved marvellous progress on the scientific and technological side, but yet they are torn by strife and they are unable to bring about peace, safety and security of their own people. It only shows that other qualities are also necessary besides those developed by science and technology.

Just now a student was introduced for his Degree and he was called Doctor of Philosophy in Science. In other words science is also regarded as a branch of philosophy. The function of the universities is not merely to send out technically skilled and professionally competent men, but it is their duty to produce in them the quality of compassion, the quality which enables the individuals to treat one another in a truly democratic spirit. Our religions have proclaimed from the very beginning that each human individual is to be regarded as a spark of the Divine. *Tat tvam asi*, that art thou, is the teaching of the Upanishads. The Buddhists declare that each individual has in him a spark of the Divine and could become a Bodhisattva. These proclamations by themselves are not enough. So long as these principles are merely clauses in the Constitution, and not functioning realities, in the daily life of the people, we are far from the ideals which we have set before ourselves. Minds and hearts of the people require to be altered. We must strive to become democratic not merely in the political sense of the term but also in the social and economic sense. It is essential to bring about this democratic change, this democratic temper, this kind of outlook by a proper study of the humanities including philosophy and religion.

There is a great verse which says that in this poison tree of *samsara* are two fruits of incomparable value. They are the enjoyment of great books and the company of good souls. If you want to absorb the fruits of great literature, well, you must read them, read them not as we do cricket stories but read them with concentration. Our generation in its rapid travel has not achieved the habit of reading the great books and has lost the habit of being influenced by the great classics of our country. If these principles of democracy in our Constitution are to become habits of mind and patterns of behaviour, principles which change the very character of the individual and the nature of the society, it can be done only by the study of great literature, of philosophy and religion. That is why even though our country needs great scientists, great technologists, great engineers, we should not neglect to make them humanists. While we retain science and technology, we must remember that science and technology are not all. We must note the famous statement that merely by becoming literate without the development of compassion we become demoniac. So no university can regard itself as a true university unless it sends out young men and women who are not only learned but whose hearts are full of compassion for suffering humanity. Unless that is there, the university education must be regarded as incomplete.

I have been a teacher for nearly all my adult life, for over forty years. I have lived with students and it hurts me very deeply when I find that the precious years during which a student has to live in the university are wasted by some of them. I do not say by all of them. Teachers and students form a family and in a family you cannot have the spirit of the trade union. Such a thing should be inconceivable in a university. University life is a cooperative enterprise between teachers and students and I do hope that the students will not do a disservice to themselves by resorting to activities which are antisocial in character.

Character is destiny. Character is that on which the destiny of a nation is built. One cannot have a great nation with men of small character. If we want to build a great nation, we must try to train a large number of young men and women who have character. We must have young men and women who look upon others as the living images of themselves as our Shastras have so often declared. But whether in public life or in student life, we cannot reach great heights if we are lacking in character. We cannot climb the mountain when the very ground at our feet is crumbling. When the very basis of our structure is shaky, how can we reach the heights which we have set before ourselves? We must all have humility. Here is a country which we are interested in building up. For whatever service we take up, we should not care for what we receive. We should know how much we can put into that service. That should be the principle which should animate our young men and women. Ours is a great country. We have had for centuries a great history. The whole of the East reflects our culture. We have to represent what India taught right from the time of Mohenjo-daro and Harappa. Whether in domestic affairs or in international affairs we must adhere to certain standards. My advice to the young men and women who are graduating today through this University is: Mother India expects of you that your lives should be clean, noble and dedicated to selfless work.

SHEILA DHAR

EXTRACT FROM *RAGA 'N JOSH*.

'. . . whenever he plays the raga Malhar,
dark clouds gather and it invariably
starts to rain.'

Playing for the Flowers

I don't know exactly when my family adopted Ustad Bundu Khan as their favourite outsider. He had always been there as far back as I can remember, lending colour, variety, and a little bit of magic to our lives, specially on occasions like the Holi festival, a wedding in the family, or even a dinner party my father sometimes threw for the cultural elite of Delhi. A *sarangi* recital by Ustad Bundu Khan usually preceded or followed the eating and drinking and was regarded as a great treat offered by our family. Not many of the invitees had specially cultivated ears but the general view was that classical music was a good thing and should be sought after. The charm of the music was greatly enhanced by my father's fabulous introductions. He tended to romanticize and mystify the greatness of the artiste, his instrument, the raga, and the treasure-house of Hindustani music in general.

'Bundu Khan used to practise so hard and so long that blood would spurt from his fingernails, but he would still go on and on until his teacher asked him to stop.' Or, 'the only way to experience the raga Malkaus is to listen to it standing in cold, knee-deep water in a river on a moonless night.' Or, 'whenever he plays the raga Malhar, dark clouds gather and it invariably starts to rain.' My father made statements of this kind with a mixture of relish and authority which was characteristic of him. Whether what he said was literally true or not seemed irrelevant. My gullible aunts, the refined guests, specially the ladies, and some of us children listened wide-eyed, hungry for more myths and accounts of incredible musical feats which spoke of dedication, beauty, and the true meaning of things. After my father's stories, the music sounded even more magical than it would otherwise have done.

We placed Bundu Khan on a pedestal and grew up almost worshipping him. The welcome he received every time he came to the house was so intense that he seemed to shrivel up a little under its impact and look even smaller and more bent than he was. But his visits to us must have been a relief from the noisy and congested environment of his own large joint family establishment in Suiwalan in the Old City. He was not really concerned about the poor living conditions. What bothered him was having to deal with the world outside music. He once told us that when he was young, he was expected to do errands in the vegetable market for his mother and aunts. 'It seemed to take forever,' he said with a tortured expression. We quite understood that the real hardship for him must have been the time he was forced to be away from music. To get over the problem, he designed a small bamboo *sarangi* which he could sling over his shoulder unobtrusively and use for practice with the fingers of his left hand without making any sound while he went about his extra-musical chores. He added that he would drape a light shawl over the left shoulder to hide the *sarangi* so that he didn't have to listen to casual comments from passing busybodies.

'I didn't want to go around telling the whole world that I was trying to perfect my finger-work. I arranged things so that they could neither see nor hear what I was doing. That way I felt quite free,' he used to say.

Bundu Khan's occasional visits gradually became a regular weekly feature. He came every Sunday when my father was home and spent the whole day playing and explaining ragas to whoever cared to listen, and even to those who did not. Most of the time my father was the core of his audience, but even when he was not Bundu Khan's enthusiasm for his art continued to overflow. He would play for whoever he sighted – a child, a servant, giggling teenagers or serious adults. And when there was no one, he happily and compulsively played for himself. He always carried his *sarangi* on his person as though it were part of his body. It was said about him that though he was a renowned artiste who had been court musician of the princely states of Rampur and Indore, he would just as happily accompany a lowly wayside villager reciting couplets from the Ramayana of Tulsidas or play at the Ramlila celebrations in the Parade Grounds in front of the Red Fort. He simply could not resist any opportunity to play, because he heard the possibility of beautiful music in everything and couldn't rest until he had found it.

One Sunday morning Bundu Khan got lost in our house. Dependable old Masoom Ali, my grandfather's chauffeur, had driven the family Dodge to Suiwalan and brought the maestro back in accordance with my father's standing instructions and deposited him on the veranda. After a few moments my father hurried out of his dressing room to greet him but he was nowhere to be seen. Not in the lavatory, not still in the car, not on the terrace, nowhere. My father's faithful valet, the smirking Jai Singh whom we all hated, was sent hunting everywhere without result. Half an hour after the panic set in we heard the faint, scratchy sounds of a *sarangi*. They seemed to be coming from the garden but we could not see anyone there. We followed my father in the direction of the sound and tracked it down to a tall, thick hedge of sweet peas that divided the huge garden in front of our house into two sections. Ustad Bundu Khan was lying in the flower bed on the farther side, his instrument balanced on his chest and shoulder, his eyes closed, completely engrossed in the music he was playing. Even my father who prided himself on courtly manners did not know how to awaken such a great musician from his reverie, or how to call out such a revered name aloud. Anyhow, with much fake coughing and embarrassed clearing of the throat, my father managed to catch his attention. Ustad Bundu Khan opened his eyes, just a slit, and scrambled to his feet when he saw the concern on the faces of the small assemblage.

'It is springtime, and I was playing for the flowers,' he said in complete explanation.

The sweet peas were indeed in full bloom and that morning, for all of us, and for ever, the perfume of these flowers became a part of Raga Bahar, which he had been playing on this occasion.

Absolute, unquestioning respect for all artistes was a very early lesson that all the children of our household imbibed. In this matter it was my father who laid down the law. We had to learn a whole new set of manners and values which were quite different from good behaviour in other social situations. The normal standards of cleanliness and elegance that one had been taught no longer applied when it came to musicians and poets. However unkempt and ragged they might be, they were automatically entitled to almost god-like reverence, the kind of reverence my grandmother unquestioningly lavished on the unimpressive, raisin-like little idol that dominated her little prayer room at one end of the long back veranda. This idol, with its tinny, painted smile was swathed in brocade robes too big for its body and was offered wonderful gifts, flowers and delicacies regularly. It was the most treasured and powerful focus of our lives. The same attitude was extended to Ustad Bundu Khan by all the sixty-odd members of the household and naturally by all the fourteen servants, regardless of whether or not they really understood the greatness of his art. My father was constantly instructing the women and children of the household in the etiquette of the mysterious world of traditional musicians. One could not stretch one's legs while sitting or change position while the music was going on. One's feet could never be visible, and even when covered could not point in the direction of the instruments. One could not speak a word, or eat or drink anything in the same room. The smallest slip could be construed as impertinence. Though fascinated by the proximity of this great master, most of the children thought the safest course was to hang their heads, crouch in a corner and pretend they did not exist.

My father did not consider this satisfactory either. It

was important to him that his family make a favourable impression. Because I was considered to be more interested in music than my cousins, the heaviest weight of my father's project of educating the entire family in the norms of hospitality fell on me. Although far from being shy, I was nonetheless mortified when I was asked to approach Ustad Bundu Khan after a music session was over and serve him tea. I must have been about fifteen years old at the time. I now know that my father wanted me to perform this act of devotion both for my own sake and also to make the point that our extraordinary guest was too special to be served by servants. My father's expectations made me nervous. I was not sure that I would have the wits to say the right thing in the right accent at the right moment.

My mother poured a cup of tea for the Ustad and handed it to me encouragingly. Her manner told me that she had absolute confidence in my ability to offer it to our eminent guest in a proper way. Ustad Bundu Khan took the cup from me with a vague smile as though it were a bird that might fly away. I brought the sugar bowl next and asked him how many spoons he wanted. He looked mystified and said in his soft, hoarse voice, 'As many as you feel like putting in; it doesn't matter.' I started to add sugar to his cup, hoping he would stop me at some point; but when he didn't, even after I had put in six teaspoons, I put the bowl down myself. From the platter of hot samosas my mother prompted me to offer next, he picked up two and thrust them into the teacup, stirring the whole mess vigorously with a teaspoon, looking into the middle distance with faintly rheumy eyes. He did the same thing to the piece of *barfi* he accepted from the serving dish of sweets that was held out to him most deferentially. By this time there was no tea left in the teacup, only a thick, gooey pulp. The liquid had squirted on to the saucer, his clothes, and the floor. He seemed quite oblivious of this, and totally indifferent to eating or drinking. He took a couple of teaspoons of the unsightly mixture in his teacup to his mouth as a sort of reflex action, muttering something about the *darja* or degree of the *komal gandhar* in Raga Darbari to my father as he did so. All the other members of the family present at the tea were gazing adoringly at him as though he had just provided yet another proof of his otherworldliness.

I remember Ustad Bundu Khan as a frail man with a lined brown face and large, soft but sunken eyes that were usually half closed and fixed dreamily at something which was visible only to him. He dressed in *chooridar* pajamas and *sherwani* like most members of his community and profession. I never saw him bare-headed. On formal occasions he donned a colourful, oversized and elaborately tied Rajasthani turban and at other times a boat-shaped cloth cap. His footwear consisted of heavy, laced, Western-style walking shoes that seemed to have no connection with him or the rest of his outfit. His ears were large and stuck out just a little. This along with his sudden, childlike smile gave him the look of a pixie. It was whispered in our household that he was an opium addict. There wasn't the slightest hint of disapproval in this. Everyone completely understood that such a man must need to escape from the tediousness of daily life somehow.

Once in a rare mood he began to talk about the rigorous training he received in his youth from his maternal uncle

Mamman Khan. The incident he described was not aimed at anyone. Perhaps he just enjoyed recalling it himself.

'I had practised fast runs in the raga Bahar for three years. Both the ascent and the descent of the raga are looped, so it is not easy to be fluent at speed. But I was determined to earn a word of praise from Mamu. I worked hard at a typical *taan* of the raga until it was perfect and then I confidently played it for him. He made a face and shook his head. It was not supple enough, he said. According to him, my *taan* in the descent was like the neck of a pig which is so thick that it cannot even look back. I went to work for another year, for several hours a day, just concentrating on the problem of the pig's neck. Finally, I managed to get it right. You see, the *taan* does not actually need to look back over its shoulder, but to be beautiful it must sound as though it could bend if it had to.'

'So, what did your Mamu say when you got it right?' my brother asked eagerly.

Ustad Bundu Khan smiled shyly, looking like a grizzled elf. 'Mamu heard me go up and down many times. Then he said "yes".'

That 'yes' was apparently the highest praise Mamu had ever bestowed on his amazing protégé. The recollection of it still made his eyes shine though there had been so much achievement and recognition in the intervening forty-five years!

It was not usual for Bundu Khan to tell anecdotes. On the whole, he could not express himself in speech at all but was most eloquent in the musical language of the *sarangi*. When he sat on the floor with his instrument, bow in hand, he was inexhaustible. He could happily demonstrate, explain and give examples of this and that all night long. Being without his *sarangi* was the only situation he considered uncomfortable. He seemed always to want the elaborate, long-winded hospitality for which our home was known to end quickly so that the business of life which for him meant the business of music could go on.

Those were times when there could be only one opinion on any matter in households like ours, though it could emanate from different sources in the family. In the matter of art and culture it was my father's opinion that prevailed. In the matter of what the women and children would wear or eat it was my grandmother's, and in all other matters my grandfather's. The reverence and awe in which Ustad Bundu Khan was held by my father was a clear signal to all, including my grandparents, the servants and the children, that they should follow his example.

This was not hard to do for anybody. He was so simple and unworldly that everyone loved him and felt protective towards him. In the 1940s, when we were in close touch with his life, it was my impression that people and organizations also valued his innocence. Nobody took advantage of him, or used him as they undoubtedly would have had he been part of the performance circuit in the music world today. His own family, his pupils, his princely patrons in Rampur and Indore, the music organizations that were springing up in Delhi and elsewhere as an expression of a new awareness of the old culture, the radio, HMV – the recording company – and the cultural elite of the big cities all treated him with unqualified deference.

Once a music circle in Allahabad invited him to perform and offered a thousand rupees as his fee in addition to travel and living expenses. He brought the original letter and the reply he had dictated to his son Umrao Khan for my father's approval. The reply said in polite Urdu, 'Unless I am paid at least five hundred and Umrao Khan is paid at least two hundred, I must refuse.' It took quite a lot of effort for my father to explain that the offer he had received was better than what he was asking for and that his son had not been mentioned at all in the invitation. Bundu Khan looked bemused, tried to count and add on the fingers of his hands but gave up after a while, his lined, childlike face wreathed in smiles.

He had the habit of breaking into song in his rough, cracked voice while he played the *sarangi*. There could not be a sharper contrast between two sounds. His bowing produced a clear, bubbling fountain of honey while his singing voice was gruff and toneless. The compulsive singing was interesting and informative when he was recollecting the *bandish* or composition and sharing the source of the music with connoisseurs in private *baithaks*, but it didn't go down so well with the radio authorities and the recording companies as it disturbed the flow of exquisite sound from his instrument. My father tactfully urged the Ustad to restrain himself during his next broadcast.

'Please, just let the *sarangi* do all the singing and explaining. Radio listeners do not really understand what you are saying,' he told him. We all gathered round the large, battered Philips radio set that stood on a corner table in the drawing room of our house to listen to our idol. I remember thrilling to the magical strains of the raga Chandni Kedara. 'You have to hear this raga on a moonlit night to get its full flavour,' my father whispered. When the programme was about to end, we exchanged smiles of relief because Ustad Bundu Khan had indeed desisted from speaking, singing and explaining in the middle of his recital as he always used to, even if it was a live broadcast. My father was deeply satisfied and took the entire credit for this bit of grooming. When the strains of the music died down after the allotted half-hour, and just before the announcer came on, we heard Bundu Khan's hoarse voice, clear and triumphant:

'See, I didn't say a word this time!' he managed to say just before he was cut off.

The partition of the country in 1947 was a terrible trauma for the Ustad who did not understand at all what had happened and why. He did not want to go anywhere, or change his life in any way. He must have been about sixty years old at this time but no one knew his age for certain. Soon after Partition, many members of his joint family went away to Pakistan, including his brothers, sisters and son. He couldn't bring himself to go, to leave the courtyard in his old family house where he had practised, played and taught for almost fifty years. So he clung to his old life for almost three years, depending for emotional support on the depleted household of cousins and nephews who had stayed behind. But we could all see the change in him. He would just come in and sit down quietly with his eyes closed as though he were dozing, instead of playing as he used to. When invited to do so, he would get into the music and drown in it completely, but this did not happen automatically as before. One day my father asked him what was bothering him, and his eyes filled with tears.

'I have tried,' he said, choking a little, 'but it is difficult. My children have gone. My wife has gone too.'

After much agonizing, he decided to uproot himself and follow his family. My father devotedly undertook to make all the arrangements for his safe travel and went to enormous trouble to ensure that he didn't have to worry about anything. I remember that he was very attached to an old radio set he had and wanted to take it, along with his large collection of *sarangis.* To arrange this was quite complicated at the time but with the help of friends in various offices and the army, my father managed to transport him quite painlessly and safely.

We never knew how he coped with his new life in Karachi. My father received only one extraordinary letter of thanks three months after his departure. He had dictated it to someone in Urdu and signed his name in his shaky, illiterate scrawl. The letter carried two sentences, the first said that he would never forget all that my father had done for him. The second was somewhat longer and said 'Here are the important *taans* of Malkaus.' About twenty note-patterns in the raga Malkaus followed. My father was so touched that he wept. He said he would never need to use the Malkaus *taans* in his life, but Ustad Bundu Khan's intention was to offer him what he considered most precious. This letter of Bundu Khan's reverberated through the remaining years of my father's life. He never tired of saying that this was the most graceful gesture he had ever come across.

We were hungry for news of Ustad Bundu Khan and used to try regularly to tune in to Radio Pakistan to catch his programmes, but never had any luck. Instead we stumbled upon many beautiful new ghazal singers who were marvellous and quite unlike anything that we had heard in India. Ustad Bundu Khan's relatives in Suiwalan said that he was doing a lot of recording for the radio in Karachi, but there were no live concerts or soirées, and that he was not very happy at the status of classical music in Pakistan. This was eating into him, they said. They must have been right because barely five years after his departure we heard that he had died. No one could tell us anything more to help us weather the blow. All we knew was that this beautiful life, which had nurtured us so long and so deeply, had been snuffed out behind a thick, black curtain.

SUBHAS CHANDRA BOSE

ADDRESS IN SINGAPORE, 1943.

'...there is no task which our women cannot undertake and no sacrifice and suffering which our women cannot undergo.'

Address to the Women's Section of the Indian Independence League, Singapore
(12 July 1943)

Sisters! I thank you with all my heart, for the warm welcome you have given me this evening. I also thank you with all my heart for your enthusiastic participation in the mammoth meeting which was held opposite the Tokku Petsu-shi Buildings. In spite of the rain you stuck to your seats till the end, and this moved me and my friends who participated in the meeting. I also know that some of you took your children there. Your bravery and enthusiasm thrilled all of us. I have the least doubt in my mind that your mission, which has started auspiciously, will grow rapidly.

You know well the service which Indian women have been rendering in the national movement during the past twenty years. From the time of India's regeneration, Indian women have been vigorously taking part in public life. This change can be clearly noticed. Since 1921, when the Congress was regenerated under Mahatma Gandhi's leadership, our sisters have performed great deeds not only in the Congress movements and the civil disobedience struggle but also in the secret revolutionary movements.

It will not be an exaggeration if I say that there are no public activities or departments of our national effort in which women are not participating. During the past many years of our national movement, women have been equal to men in undergoing suffering with joy and courage. The Indian women never lagged behind anybody in going from village to village, without food and water, addressing meeting after meeting, in carrying the message of freedom from house to house, in conducting election campaigns, in taking out processions in spite of the Government's bans and in the face of lathi charge by the merciless British police, and in putting up with the privations of prison life, torture and humiliations. Last but not least, our heroic sisters also took an active part in the secret revolutionary activities. Many a time they have demonstrated that they, too, if necessary, could use firearms as well as their brothers.

When I express my confidence that you are today prepared to fight and suffer for the sake of your motherland, I do not mean only to cajole you with empty words. I know the capabilities of our womanhood well. I can, therefore, say with certainty that there is no task which our women cannot undertake and no sacrifice and suffering which our women cannot undergo.

The time for launching the final campaign to liberate

our motherland has now come. Only very rarely such opportunities occur in a nation's life. Surely such an opportunity will not come again in our lifetime, nor even in the next hundred years. Only by God's grace have we got such an opportunity. If we seize it and sacrifice our all, we can surely liberate our country.

I know some among us have been thinking that British imperialism was immortal and had no end. But I know that history wills it otherwise. History has taught us that every empire will fall in the same way as it has arisen. Similarly, the time has now come for the exit of British imperialism from the world. We have seen with our own eyes the destruction of the British Empire in this part of the world. We are also going to witness its disappearance from India and other parts of the world.

Some years back I read a book on the British Empire by an Englishman named Meredith Conrad. Referring to India, he says that once the Indians become united, the British will not be able to rule over them. He has further said that the empire which came into being in a day will die in a night.

I have mentioned in my broadcast that it took just seven days to drive them out of the stronghold of Singapore, which they had built in the course of twenty years. Of course, I do not expect that the British can be driven out of India within a week. But you can mathematically calculate how many weeks it will take to drive out the British once we launch our final military action.

Sisters! I think every one of you believes that the time to begin our efforts for our salvation has come now. I also sincerely believe that you all wish this war to end in the defeat of Anglo-American imperialism, because India can gain her freedom only if it is vanquished. It is for this reason that I have often been saying that the liberation of India is dependent on the victory of the Axis Powers. Today India and the Axis Powers are facing a common enemy. We, therefore, have a common goal. We have to fight against our common foe; we should be prepared to make any sacrifice and win our freedom by sharing the joys and sorrows equally among ourselves.

If we get freedom without sacrifice and suffering, it will be of no avail, because we will not be able to preserve the freedom which is gained so easily. We shall therefore get our freedom only through our suffering. I firmly believe that we can give adequate support to our motherland by our total mobilization.

Therefore, sisters, you too must take your share in the coming struggle. You can serve in various capacities. Women have special skill in some specific fields. For example, you can serve in the hospitals. When our military campaigns have started, who will take care of our wounded soldiers? Will it not be shameful if our sisters do not come forward to comfort our wounded soldiers? Sisters, this is only a part of your duty. You can also help us in the recruitment of soldiers and collection of funds and supplies. Sometimes you may even have to take up arms.

To those who say that it will not be proper for our women to carry guns, my only request is that they look into the pages of our history. What brave deeds the Rani of Jhansi performed during the First War of Independence in 1857! Similarly, many brave women like the Rani of Jhansi are required in our Last War of Independence also. It is not important how many guns you can carry or how many cartridges you can fire. It is the spiritual force which will be generated by your heroic example that is important. Indians – both common people and members of the British Indian army – who are on the border areas of India, will, on seeing you march with guns on your shoulders, voluntarily come forward to receive the guns from you and carry on the struggle started by you. I do not have the least doubt about this. Therefore, I can say with certainty that the time has come for every Indian – man and woman, boy and girl – to come forward and make great sacrifices for liberating India.

Sisters, your energetic activities will not only inspire our countrymen living in Malaya, East Asia and Syonan but also those living within our country. I have no doubt that the 388 million Indians, on hearing about your efforts and your preparations for the fight, will be greatly inspired. I wish all your efforts are crowned with success. Your task is the same as ours. In this common task, in this struggle, in this suffering and sacrifice, all of us – without any distinction of man or woman, boy or girl, poor or rich, young or old – should stand shoulder to shoulder, should start the final struggle and should hasten the day of India's deliverance.

I once again thank you for the welcome you have given me today and for your enthusiastic participation in the public meeting the other day. I also thank you for the purse you have presented me today. I wish that all your activities for the liberation of our motherland end in victory.

As I told you earlier, the time for preparing ourselves for the final struggle has come. I have already announced to the world the formation of the Azad Hind Army. It is preparing itself for the war of liberation. I hope that the time will come for me to announce to the world that the Jhansi Rani Regiment also is preparing for the struggle. This work should be started immediately. I, therefore, request all those who want to join the Jhansi Rani Regiment to come forward and give your names.

SUBROTO BAGCHI

EXTRACT FROM *MBA AT 16.*

'Many of us can walk well when the path is shown, but very few can create a path where none exists.'

Kamya Goes Solar

Kamya Swaminathan's mother studied business and specialized in finance at Harvard. When the family returned to India, she did not want to work for the for-profit sector. She wanted to channelize her knowledge into addressing urgent social issues and chose to work with the Azim Premji Foundation. The family often got together to discuss interlinked social issues like poverty and education. 'The poor are poor because they are poor,' said her mom one day. Kamya was completely baffled.

She went on to explain the concept of the 'vicious cycle of poverty,' first propounded by economist E.F. Schumacher, who left a lasting impact on the world with his ideas on what the developing world really needed as against what the West propagated. Schumacher felt that efforts to alleviate poverty usually fail because the poor are always trapped in a vicious cycle. Consider this: A man is poor. So he has no savings. Because he has no assets, he cannot offer collateral or a mortgage to get a bank loan. Because a bank will not give him a loan, he cannot start a business or improve his condition in any way. As a result, he stays poor. That was amazingly simple and explained why, for centuries, large parts of Asia, Africa and South America have remained in conditions of misery.

'So, to uplift someone from poverty, one has to break the vicious cycle at some point,' explained Kamya's mom. One way is for the poor people to form 'cooperatives', where a number of poor people come together to solve their own economic problems with small amounts of money. The cooperative movement actually spread quite a bit in the last century and that is how we saw the emergence of many significant cooperative efforts, some of which became hugely successful. One of them is India's White Revolution led by the legendary Verghese Kurien, who made Amul a household name via Operation Flood. The success of Amul transformed India from a milk-deficient country to a milk-surplus one, within the span of a generation. India's milk production was lagging behind demand because most households in the villages had only one cow or buffalo. They could not carry their meagre milk production to big cities and towns. So they sold it to middlemen who swindled them. In came Kurien, who asked the individual producers to come together and form cooperatives – when a large number of milk farmers came together and collected their individual production in one place, suddenly it was not small any more. Individually, they were insignificant. Collectively, they were significant enough for a milk tanker to come all the way to their village and pick up the production, eliminating the middleman who not only exploited the villagers economically but also perpetrated other injustices. This story has been touchingly told by film-maker Shyam Benegal in *Manthan* ('The Churning'). So, when the villagers formed what came to be known as a milk cooperative, they could extend its power to strike bargains in buying everything, from their own day-to-day needs to fodder for their cattle. As a country, within decades, India transformed.

The cooperative movement transformed individuals, families and villages wherever it worked well. Not all cooperatives did. But, by and large, the idea of cooperatives worked for the poor but not for the poorest of the poor. They remained outside the boundaries of economic activity, trapping them in a state of endless misery. Until an economist named Mohammad Yunus arrived on the scene in Bangladesh, after its independence from Pakistan in 1971.

Yunus did not have to study economics to know poverty. He was born to a poor family, in a poor village, in a poor country. Despite the debilitating poverty and his mother's mental illness, the young Yunus pursued his education well enough to earn a Fulbright scholarship and get to the US. There he finished with a doctorate from Vanderbilt University and became an assistant professor at Middle Tennessee State University. He could have lived a comfortable American life but his call of duty came when Bangladesh broke away from Pakistan. The war-ravaged country needed reconstruction and, at the behest of Professor Nurul Islam, another economist who headed Bangladesh's planning commission, Yunus returned to serve his motherland. He had worked as a research assistant with Islam before leaving for the US.

The return to the motherland was not easy. To begin with, Yunus found the government job boring. He quit and went back to teaching, this time at the University of Chittagong. Shortly after, in 1974, Bangladesh witnessed a terrible famine. As things worsened, Yunus felt a deep inner compulsion to get involved. He was not a rich man who could solve the problem with money. He was an economist and he needed to fix the issue of economic deprivation at the level of an equation first.

According to him, the poor could not get access to capital because, over centuries, banking institutions had been trained to lend money in certain defined ways. They lent money to people who already had enough and could provide collaterals, because the lenders were always looking for safety. They tried to protect themselves via elaborate paperwork and lawyers. And they gave out large sums; they did not like to lend tiny amounts. The cost of managing debt via the required amount of paperwork and the cost of recovery remained the same whether you lent a hundred or a million. So large banks liked large borrowers.

Poor people invariably needed tiny amounts at a time, enough to buy, say, a cartload of vegetables that they could sell over the next couple of days. They were not literate, so they had no use for paperwork and because they were poor, they could give no collateral. But they had honourable intentions – if someone was willing to loan them small amounts, they would put it to work, earn some more and return the principal with interest so that they could borrow some more when the need arose. Banks were not trained to deal with such people.

Yunus discovered another interesting thing, early in his experiment with what came to be known as micro-credit: this happened well before his Grameen Bank became a household name in Bangladesh. He found that when he loaned a small amount of money to a poor man and a similar amount to a poor woman, the woman was more likely to put the money to productive use and, as a result of that, return to repay the debt. In villages, the women had a stronger sense of responsibility for their family – the men did not care as much. They were more prone to blowing the money away and return to the vicious cycle of poverty.

So Yunus took out a small amount from his meagre personal resources and lent it in even smaller amounts to a group of women, and that is how the miracle of micro-credit was born. The women formed a support group, helping each other stay the course in putting the money to productive use. They earned some money by selling something or buying poultry or a cow or a goat that they could use as a regenerative source of income. They also introduced new members to the group, thereby providing personal guarantee for new borrowers. The money earned as interest was lent to these newer borrowers. The pool of money grew, the borrowers grew, they all started building thousands of small businesses and the idea led to the formation of the Grameen Bank.

Bangladesh is one of the world's poorest and most populous countries even today. Being poor in Bangladesh is not just about economics and politics but also about religion. Being an Islamic nation, clerics threatened the women borrowers that they would be refused a Muslim burial because borrowing and lending money for interest is prohibited in Islam. Yunus persisted in his efforts and, by 2007, Grameen Bank had lent a staggering 6.38 billion dollars to 7.4 million small borrowers. He and his people had developed Grameen Bank into a globally admired model of poverty alleviation by treating the poor with respect. In 2006, the Nobel Peace Prize was awarded jointly to Yunus and the Grameen Bank.

***

Just as Mohammad Yunus was quietly creating an economic miracle with the poor in Bangladesh with his social enterprise, in Tamil Nadu in India, a doctor named Govindappa Venkataswamy – better known as Dr V – was creating a miracle in healthcare through his social enterprise, Aravind Eye Hospital.

Dr V was born in Vadamalapuram village in Tamil Nadu in 1918 to a poor household. In a film titled *Infinite Vision*, he recounts how, as a child, he had to tend to the family buffalo every morning before heading to school. As a child, he once heard that a young woman in the village had died while delivering her baby. He decided to become a doctor and save people from such untimely deaths. He studied to be an obstetrician and joined the army. Fate had other designs though. He contracted a rare form of arthritis that caused his fingers and toes to get misshapen. The army let go of him. He could no longer do the work he was trained for. Undeterred, he retrained himself as an ophthalmologist and spent all his working life as an eye surgeon in Madurai. When he was fifty-eight, Dr V was asked to retire from his government service as per rules. Instead of taking it easy, Dr V decided to start an eleven-bed eye hospital with the avowed goal of fighting 'needless blindness'. India has the largest number of blind people in the world. In 1977, Dr V estimated the number at 12 million and, according to him, 80 per cent of it was needless because it was caused by cataract. Timely detection and surgical intervention could help people to lead normal, healthy lives. But in rural India, where most of these people lived, there was the terrible nexus of poverty, ignorance and, of course, lack of affordable healthcare cost was the biggest hurdle.

Dr V had great admiration for the fast-food company McDonald's' business model, which had delivered billions of burgers across the world systematically, efficiently. When you produce things in high volume and at increased efficiency, you reduce costs and, thereby, unit prices. When prices come down, demand increases! That has been true of many things, from the personal computer to the cell phone to low-cost air travel and healthcare.

Dr V made the analogy that the sheer volume of eye patients in India meant that, with efficiency, it was possible to lower the cost per surgical procedure. And he did precisely that. Aravind Eye Hospital became the first hospital in the world to experiment with an assembly line approach to eye surgery. It used fixed assets like operating theatre and equipment on a three-shift basis so their utilization and, hence, recovery of fixed costs went up. Today, from an eleven-bed hospital, Aravind has spread into multiple facilities across India. In 2009, they treated 2.5 million people and conducted 3,00,000 operations. As many as two-thirds of all outpatients and three-fourths of all those operated upon did not have to pay anything!

One of the major causes of rural blindness is ignorance. Many people progressively lose sight because they do not know that their condition is treatable. Many do not have the means to undertake travel to a centre for treatment by themselves or may not have someone to take them there. For a person accompanying the patient, it means a loss of daily wage. So Aravind introduced buses that went from village to village with doctors who examined patients on site; the buses would then bring those requiring surgery to the centre and drop them back after recovery! Initially, Aravind had to import expensive intra-ocular lenses that were needed to restore normal vision after the surgery. Each cost over 100 dollars apiece. Over time, and with volumes, they could produce lenses themselves for less than 5 dollars apiece. Today, they actually export lenses!

***

'Has it ever occurred to you that it is the poor people in this world who live in greater darkness?' Kamya's mother asked her, as the two sat out in the balcony, looking at the city lights flickering on in the horizon. It was a magical moment and Kamya loved it – how the lights came on in ones and twos and you could count them and then they went viral and, before you knew it, the city was aglow, awash in a surreal luminosity.

'I know what you mean, Ma. Illiteracy and poverty go hand in hand and, because of that, the poor who have no access to education get disenfranchised, are denied opportunities and live in a state of darkness of the mind.'

'No, not darkness of the mind but real darkness,' said Ma. Kamya couldn't comprehend her mother's thoughts but she realized that she was about to share something important. Kamya sat there, in the twilit balcony, waiting to be enlightened about real darkness.

Access to on-demand lighting is a privilege of position and power everywhere in the world. How much light you consume is dependent on how well off your parents are! A young man named Harish Hande realized this during his studies towards a doctorate at the University of Massachusetts in Boston, USA. That is how he eventually got interested in solar energy at that time. He had a chance to visit the Dominican Republic where, for the first time, he saw the connection between poverty and darkness. His heart bled and he decided to devote his life to bringing affordable energy to the poor. He then spent time in Sri Lanka, in a village where no one spoke English, to get a grip of rural needs and challenges. He developed solar solutions for the rural folk, not through the lens of the city dweller. For instance, he provided solutions for unusual needs like keeping rampaging elephants at bay! In the Sri Lankan village, the locals told him that the critical need was not heating or lighting but it was to keep elephants at bay, who came in herds at night, destroyed crops and huts and sometimes killed people. Harish created solar-charged electric fences to save life and property.

Eventually, he returned to India to set up SELCO, now a four-million-dollar enterprise that continuously researches unique lighting applications to significantly improve the conditions of the rural and urban poor.

Consider a roadside vegetable vendor. The poor woman opens shop to catch the evening traffic, commuting home from work. Within a few hours, the place is engulfed in darkness and people do not stop by to shop for vegetables any longer. At times, her vegetables perish. Imagine her loss. Harish's team built a solar battery charging solution that created multiple economic opportunities. A man started the business of renting solar-charged car batteries. He loaded them in an autorickshaw every evening and rented the batteries for twenty-five rupees an evening to the vegetable sellers. When dusk fell, the solar lights came on, adding at least two business hours and facilitating significant economic benefits for the vendors. Every small entrepreneur's livelihood needs are unique. The needs of cobblers are different from, say, those of farmers. For each specific need, SELCO's Application R&D team builds a unique and affordable solution based on the principle that it must pay for itself and increase the earning potential of the user from the word go.

Harish could have taken up any lucrative job in a well-paying corporation anywhere in the world. Yet, despite great initial difficulty, with immense perseverance, he built his social enterprise to bring economic value to people who exist at the base of the economic pyramid. His work requires that he spend most of his time in India. He has made a huge personal sacrifice to be where his work is – leaving his wife and two children in the US. He sees them for a few months every year but he feels that the poor and the needy customers of SELCO are his family as well. He has received several honours, including the United Nations Development Programme's Social Enterpreneur of the Year Award in 2007, and spoken about his work at global platforms such as the World Economic Forum in Davos, where leaders congregate annually to learn from each other and ascertain trends. In 2011, Harish was honoured with the prestigious Ramon Magsaysay Award.

From Steve Jobs to Harish Hande, from entrepreneurs who build for-profit companies to those who build social enterprises, there is a common streak. All these people are 'path creators.' Many of us can walk well when the path is shown, but very few can create a path where none exists. That is the stuff entrepreneurs are made of. Whether they are born with it or they acquire the ability as they go along, we really do not know.

The illuminated city of Bangalore no longer engaged Kamya's young mind. As she sat listening to her mother in rapt attention, she was thinking of the vast divide between the haves and the have-nots of the world and how one day she had to make her bit.

SUDHA MURTY

EXTRACT FROM *HOW I TAUGHT MY GRANDMOTHER TO READ AND OTHER STORIES.*

'At the bottom there was a small line: "Lady candidates need not apply".'

'Appro J.R.D.'

There are two photographs that hang on my office wall. Every day when I enter my office I look at them and start my day. They are pictures of two old people. One is of a gentleman in a blue suit and the other one is a black and white photograph of an old man with dreamy eyes and a white beard.

Many people have asked me if they are related to me. Some people have even asked me, 'Is this black and white photo that of a Sufi saint or a religious guru?'

I smile and reply, 'No, nor are they related to me.'

'Then why do you look at them and start the day?'

'These people made an impact on my life. I am grateful to them.'

'Who are these people?'

'The man in the blue suit is Bharat Ratna J.R.D. Tata and the black and white photo is of Sir Jamsetji Tata.'

'But why do you have their photos in your office?'

'You can call it gratitude.'

Then, invariably, I have to tell the person the following

story. It happened a long time ago. I was young and bright, bold and idealistic. I was studying in the final year for my Master's degree in computer science at Indian Institute of Science, Bangalore, which was then known as the Tata Institute. For me, life was full of fun and joy. I did not know what helplessness or injustice meant.

It was probably the April of 1974. Bangalore was just becoming warm. Red *gulmohars* were blooming at the IISc campus. I was the only girl in my postgraduate department in Engineering, and was staying in the ladies' hostel. Other girls were pursuing their research in different departments of science.

After completing my postgraduation, I was keen to go abroad to do my doctorate in computer science and had already been offered scholarships from universities in USA. I had not thought of taking up a job in India.

One day, while on the way to my hostel from the lecture hall, I saw an advertisement on the noticeboard.

It was a standard job-requirement notice from the famous automobile company TELCO.* It stated that the company required young, bright engineers, hard-working, with excellent academic background, etc.

At the bottom there was a small line: 'Lady candidates need not apply'.

I read it and was very upset. For the first time, I was faced with gender discrimination.

Though I was not keen on taking up a job, I took it as a challenge and decided to apply. I had done extremely well in my studies, probably better than most of the boys. Little

* *Now Tata Motors.*

did I know then that in real life, to be successful, academic excellence is not a necessary condition.

After reading the notice, I went fuming to my room. There I decided not only to apply for the job, but also to inform the topmost person of the management of TELCO about the injustice. I got a postcard and started to write. But there was a problem. Who was the head of TELCO? I did not know. I was so ignorant that I thought it must be one of the Tatas. I knew J.R.D. Tata was the head of the Tata Group. I had seen his pictures in newspapers. Actually, Sumant Moolgaokar was then its chairman, which I was not aware of.

I took the postcard and started writing. Even now, I clearly remember what I had written to J.R.D.

'Tatas have always been pioneers. They are the people who started the basic infrastructure industries in India like iron and steel, chemicals, textiles, locomotives, etc. They have cared for higher education in India since 1900, and are responsible for the establishment of the Indian Institute of Science! Fortunately I study there. But I am surprised that in such a company you can make a distinction between men and women.'

I posted the letter that was written in anger, and after a few days forgot about it.

Within ten days, I received a telegram stating that I had to appear for an interview at TELCO Pune, at their expense. I was taken aback. But my hostel-mates told me I had to use the opportunity to go to Pune free of cost. And the reason? Pune saris were cheap! I was told to buy saris for them. I even collected thirty rupees per head for each of their saris. Now, when I look back, I feel like laughing at the reasons, but then they seemed good ones to make a trip.

This was my first visit to Pune. I fell in love with the city and even to this date it is very dear to my heart. I feel as much at home in Pune as I do at Hubli. The city changed my life in so many ways.

As directed, I went to TELCO's Pimpri office for the interview. There were six people on the panel and it was only then that I realized this was serious business.

'This is the girl who wrote to J.R.D.,' I heard them whisper to each other as soon as I entered. By then I knew for sure that I would not get a job. And when I wouldn't get a job, why should I be scared? So I was rather cool for the interview.

Even before they started the interview I knew they were biased, so I told them, rather rudely, 'I hope this is only a technical interview.'

They were taken aback by my rudeness, and even today I am ashamed of my attitude.

During the interview they asked many technical questions and I answered all of them. Then one elderly gentleman with an affectionate voice told me, 'Do you know why we said that lady candidates need not apply? The reason is that to this day we have not employed any ladies on the shop floor of the factory. This is an automobile industry. Trainees may have to work in shifts. For training, we may have to send them to Jamshedpur in Bihar. All our plants have men and machinery. Our trainees may have to drive. We have a trainee's hostel and a guesthouse for them. If a lady enters, then how can we accommodate her? We do not know how men on the shop floor will accept her. How will she come for shifts? We care for our employees, particularly if she is a lady. It is not a college where there is no gender difference. This is a factory. When it comes to academics, you are a first ranker throughout. We appreciate that. People like you should work more in research laboratories.'

I was a young girl from small-town Hubli. My world was very small. I did not know the ways of large corporate houses and their difficulties. So I answered, 'But somewhere you must start. Otherwise a lady will never be able to work in the factories. You are pioneers in many aspects of life. When I look at your industries, you are far ahead of other people. If you think this way, then how will any lady ever enter this so-called man's domain?'

'Training a candidate costs a lot to our company. You are of a marriageable age. After your training you will leave this company and shift to wherever your husband works. Is it not a waste of money for us?'

I thought for a moment and replied, 'I definitely agree with what you say. I am sure when many of you married, your wives came along with you. That has been our tradition. But is it also not true that many men undergo training, and just for a few more hundred rupees, they shift their jobs. You don't have any rule for them. You can't stop them.'

Finally, after a long interview, I was told I had been successful in securing a job at TELCO. On the way back, I got down at Hubli, my home town. I was eager to meet my father, always my best friend, and tell him my adventure. I was sure he would be happy and praise me.

But I was in for a shock. He was very upset. He said, 'You should have basic manners when addressing elderly people like J.R.D. Tata. You should have written the letter more politely and put it in an envelope, instead of sending a postcard. Now you have to take up this job because you are morally responsible.'

That is what my future had in store for me. Never ever had I thought I would take up a job at Pune. There I met a shy young man from Karnataka, we became good friends and got married.

The elderly gentleman who interviewed me was Dr Sathya Murty, who was an excellent technocrat and human being. I worked with him for some years. After joining TELCO, I realized who J.R.D. was. He was the uncrowned king of Indian industry. I did not get to meet him until I was transferred to Bombay. J.R.D. had an office at Bombay House, the headquarters of Tata Industries.

One day, I was supposed to show some reports to our chairman Mr Moolgaokar, whom everyone always referred to as SM. So I went to his office on the first floor of Bombay House.

While I was in SM's room, J.R.D. walked in. That was the first time I saw 'Appro J.R.D.'. 'Appro' means 'ours' in Gujarati. In Bombay House, people used to affectionately call him 'Appro J.R.D.'.

By this time, I knew who he was and was feeling very nervous, remembering my rude postcard to him.

SM introduced me very nicely, 'Jeh, look, this young girl is an engineer and that too a postgraduate. She has worked on the shop floor at TELCO. Is it not unusual? She was the first girl in our TELCO shop floor.'

J.R.D. looked at me. I was praying he would not ask me any questions regarding my interview or the postcard.

Thankfully he didn't ask me anything about that. Instead he remarked, 'It is nice that in our country girls are getting into engineering. By the way, what is your name?'

'When I joined TELCO, I was Sudha Kulkarni, Sir. Now I am Sudha Murty.'

'Where do you work?'

'At Nanavati Mahalaya,' I replied.

He smiled at me, nodding his head, and the two men started their discussion. I just ran out of the room.

After that I used to see J.R.D. on and off. He was the chairman of a large group of companies and I was only an engineer in one of those companies. There was nothing we had in common. I used to look at him with awe.

One day I was waiting for Murthy to come and pick me up after office hours. To my surprise, I saw J.R.D. standing next to me. I did not know how to react. I was feeling uneasy. Again I started worrying about the postcard. Now when I look back, I realize J.R.D. must have forgotten about it. It must have been a very small incident to him but not so for me.

He asked me, 'Young lady, why are you here? Office time is over.' I said, 'Sir, I am waiting for my husband to come and pick me up.'

J.R.D. said, 'It is getting dark. There's no one in the corridor. I will wait with you until your husband comes.'

I was quite used to waiting for Murthy so I was not bothered much by having to wait in the dark. But having J.R.D. waiting along with me made me very uncomfortable. Out of the corner of my eye, I looked at him.

He wore a simple white pant and shirt. He was old yet his face was glowing, without any air of superiority.

I was thinking, 'Look at this person. He is the chairman, a well-respected man in our country and he is waiting for the sake of an ordinary lady employee.'

As soon as I saw Murthy, I rushed out.

J.R.D. called and said, 'Young lady, tell your husband never to be late and make his wife wait.'

In 1982, I had to resign from my job at TELCO. I was very reluctant to resign but did not have a choice. Even now, my love and respect for the House of Tatas is the same. I always looked up to J.R.D. as my role model for his simplicity, generosity, kindness and the care he took of his employees.

After I had made my final settlements with the company, I was coming down the steps of Bombay House when I saw J.R.D. coming up. He was absorbed in some thought. I wanted to say goodbye to him. So I stopped. He saw me and he also stopped.

Gently he said, 'So what are you doing, Ms Kulkarni?' (That was the way he always addressed me.)

'Sir, I am leaving TELCO.'

'Where are you going?'

'Pune, Sir. My husband is starting a company called Infosys. So I have to shift to Pune.'

'Oh! What will you do when you are successful?'

'Sir, I do not know whether we will be successful or not.'

'Never start with diffidence. Always start with confidence. When you are successful, you must give back to society. Society gives us so much, we must return it. I wish you all the best.

Then J.R.D. continued walking up the stairs. I stood for a while, watching him. That was the last time I saw him alive.

Many years later, I met Ratan Tata in the same Bombay office occupying the same chair as J.R.D. I told him many of my sweet memories of working with TELCO. I said, 'I cannot call you Mr Tata like Murthy calls you. You are occupying "Appro J.R.D.'s" seat. You will always be "Chairman Sir" to me.'

Later, he wrote to me, 'It was nice listening about Jeh from you. The sad part is that he is not alive today to see you.'

I consider J.R.D. a great man because, in spite of being an extremely busy person, he valued one postcard written by a young girl, who was asking for justice and questioning him. He must have received thousands of letters everyday. He could have thrown mine away in a dustbin. But he didn't do that. He respected the intentions of that unknown girl, who had neither influence nor money and gave her an opportunity to work in his company. He did not merely give her a job, but also changed her life and mindset forever.

Today, in any engineering college I see that forty to fifty per cent of the students are girls. On the shop floor of many mechanical industries we see so many ladies working. That time I think of J.R.D. fondly.

If at all time stops and asks me what I want from life, I would say I wish J.R.D. were alive today to see how the company we started has grown. He would have enjoyed it wholeheartedly.

SWAMI VIVEKANANDA

The Chicago Speech, 1893.

'I am proud to belong to a religion which has taught the world both tolerance and universal acceptance.'

At the Parliament of the World's Religions

Chicago, USA | 11 September, 1893

Sisters and Brothers of America,

It fills my heart with joy unspeakable to rise in response to the warm and cordial welcome which you have given us.

I thank you in the name of the most ancient order of monks in the world; I thank you in the name of the mother of religions; and I thank you in the name of the millions and millions of Hindu people of all classes and sects.

My thanks, also, to some of the speakers on this platform who, referring to the delegates from the Orient, have told you that these men from far-off nations may well claim the honour of bearing to different lands the idea of toleration.

I am proud to belong to a religion which has taught the world both tolerance and universal acceptance. We believe not only in universal toleration, but we accept all religions as true.

I am proud to belong to a nation which has sheltered the

persecuted and the refugees of all religions and all nations of the earth.

I am proud to tell you that we have gathered in our bosom the purest remnant of the Israelites, who came to the southern India and took refuge with us in the very year in which their holy temple was shattered to pieces by Roman tyranny.

I am proud to belong to the religion which has sheltered and is still fostering the remnant of the grand Zoroastrian nation.

I will quote to you, brethren, a few lines from a hymn which I remember to have repeated from my earliest boyhood, which is every day repeated by millions of human beings:

'As the different streams having their sources in different places all mingle their water in the sea, so, O Lord, the different paths which men take through different tendencies, various though they appear, crooked or straight, all lead to Thee.'

The present convention, which is one of the most august assemblies ever held, is in itself a vindication, a declaration to the world, of the wonderful doctrine preached in the Gita:

'Whosoever comes to Me, through whatsoever form, I reach him; all men are struggling through paths which in the end lead to Me.'

Sectarianism, bigotry, and its horrible descendant, fanaticism, have long possessed this beautiful earth. They have filled the earth with violence, drenched it often and often with human blood, destroyed civilization, and sent whole nations to despair. Had it not been for these horrible demons, human society would be far more advanced than it is now.

But their time has come; and I fervently hope that the bell that tolled this morning in honour of this convention may be the death-knell of all fanaticism, of all persecutions with the sword or with the pen, and of all uncharitable feelings between persons wending their way to the same goal.

VALMIK THAPAR

EXTRACT FROM *EXOTIC ALIENS: THE LION AND THE CHEETAH IN INDIA*.

'. . . the Indian lion was never a native species or subspecies but had always been an exotic import that had been shipped into the country and bred for sport.'

In The Courts of Emperors

When I first saw the so-called Asiatic lions in the mid-1990s in Gir, their behaviour resembled that of large dogs. As I walked along a path with a forest guard, watching them from a few feet away, other guards hissed, hooted and mimicked endless varieties of domestic livestock to attract their attention. The spectacle did not even remotely resemble what I expected to see when it came to encountering wild lions. Indeed, I do not think I have ever seen a more disappointing sight in the wild. The tameness of these animals made me recall images of lions stuffed with opium (and wild asses) until they were lethargic enough to be slaughtered by Mughal emperors for sport. I then had to wait several years to see the lion in Kenya. That experience was exactly the opposite – I wouldn't have dared to get out of the relative safety of my vehicle, let alone walk around them. In the Masai Mara, I saw more than a hundred different lions in ten days. These were 'real' lions and not the caricatures I had encountered in Gir.

The suspicion that had been sown in my mind during my research for *Tiger Fire* . . . now emerged as full-blown theory. It was clear to me by now, through the books I had consulted as well as my encounters on the ground, that the Indian lion was never a native species or subspecies but had always been an exotic import that had been shipped into the country and bred for sport. As there is no conclusive genetic evidence to prove or disprove this thesis, I've had to necessarily rely on the historical record and my own training as a naturalist.

Let's start with habitat. This country's dry, moist and evergreen forests make for a very unwelcome terrain for lions, especially given the presence of tigers, the more powerful predator. Even where there are grasslands or bush (the lion's natural habitat), I couldn't imagine them eating or feasting as a pride on cinkara and blackbuck. Maybe nilgai, the largest Indian antelope, could have been suitable prey for the lion, but if that was the case, why were there hardly any records of encounters between the nilgai and the lion? The fact remains that if the nilgai was not the lion's natural prey, the country simply did not have the millions of blackbucks that would have been needed for 'indigenous' lions and cheetahs to feed on. In Africa, however, there are more than 40 species of antelope of different sizes as well as zebras, giraffes, wildebeest, wild buffaloes and warthogs – plenty of prey for the lion, which is why it flourishes in that continent. It was also odd that there were so few records of encounters with prides of lion in this country; in Africa, a pride can consist of as many as 30 animals.

What is apparent on the ground is true of the historical record as well. Romila Thapar and Yusuf Ansari have dealt with the lions in antiquity and in the Islamic and Mughal eras, but some of the points they make bear reiterating. The Mohenjo-daro seals do not depict the lion, nor do early cave paintings that date back 5,000–8,000 years ago, whereas the tiger is to be encountered everywhere. Some observers argue that the lion was a late entrant into the subcontinent, and that it only arrived on the scene 2,000–3,000 years BCE. I find that difficult to imagine because it is inconceivable that lions could have swum across the Indus (unlike tigers, they hate water) to make a home for themselves in the plains of Delhi and Haryana. Moreover, experts have testified that there '[existed] absolutely no proof of the occurrence of lions' in Afghanistan and Baluchistan – regions that bordered India. If this was indeed the case, how could wild lions have migrated into the subcontinent without passing through lands that lay just across the border? The only explanation that fits . . . is that the lion was imported into the country in large numbers and bred for release into the designated hunting grounds of Indian royals.

We have evidence of traffic in live lions from approximately the third century BCE up until the fifth century CE (especially towards Rome from different regions of Africa, much as tigers were sent from India) but for all we know, the trade in lions went back much further than that because the animal has been associated with royalty from time immemorial, and had, therefore, always been in demand. As Thomas Allsen writes:

> Ali Akbar Khitai, a Persian merchant who wrote an invaluable book on China in 1516–17, says that Muslim traders travelling overland often brought lions (*shir*) and other cats to China where they fetched a good price... The lion in China far from the natural range, had from the beginning great symbolic power.

Another clue as to the origin and place of the lion has to do with the fact that from Alexander's times (third century BCE), accounts of the animal have often talked about how tame it was. Should we take this to mean that throughout its history in the subcontinent it has always been captive, tamed, fed, trained and then sometimes hunted? We know that in the twentieth century when the lion had almost become extinct, the Nawab of Junagadh decided to manage the population in Gir (his then designated hunting ground) through intensive artificial feeding and protection. Did the Mughal emperors do the same in their time? Was the 'Royal Lion House' a breeding and holding station to train lions for the court and release them into the stage-managed hunting grounds of the emperors? If Jahangir boasted 100 lions in his court, how many did he have in his stables?

***

We know many ancient cultures set great store by the lion because it was emblematic of royalty; in this, they were merely following in the path of a well-known historical tradition.

> It was because men dreaded the lion that he became the emblem of wisdom in Assyrian sculpture and the type of courage in Hebrew poetry; that his head crowns the body of an Egyptian god, and that his form has been taken as a royal cognizance in the East and West. For no other cause is it that death is the penalty for anyone but a ruler to wear his claws in Zululand, or that among the Algerian Arabs his whole body possesses magic virtues.

Indeed, it is hard to find a culture in which the lion was not revered by the ruling class. It was deified by the people of the East – a part of the pantheon of gods in Mesopotamia, it was also considered sacred in Phoenicia. Leontopolis and Heliopolis in Egypt were central to the cult of the lion; in Amun Ra's temple at Heliopolis, 'lions were tended carefully by high ranking priests who bathed them in perfumed water, salved them, burnt incense for them and fed . . . them the choicest tidbits to the strain of sacred music.' So much so that laws were made decreeing a public mourning on the death of one of these animals, which would then be 'embalmed and entombed with great ceremony.' The lion was closely associated with the goddess Cybele – whom the Romans knew as Magna Mater – and tamed lions were kept in temples built for her. 'In ancient Greece the priests of Cybele who wandered across the country like mendicant monks, frequently had a lion with them, and made use of it in their exorcising rituals.'

Just like Mughal emperors, the pharaohs liked to appear in public in the company of tame lions; even when Ramesses II went to battle, he was accompanied by a lion that ran alongside his chariot and knocked down anyone who tried to approach the ruler. In peacetime, too, lions were constant companions to emperors and kings. Tame lions were kept at Leontopolis, the lion city in the Nile delta and near modern-day Cairo, where they were propitiated.

> Because of their long association with royalty, with royal crests, valour and so forth, there was never any challenge to the lion's status as King of the Beasts. In the hierarchy that was the animal kingdom (as then perceived), the lion's right to the title went without question.

In Baghdad, the Abbasid Caliphate would impress guests with 100 lions suitably collared and muzzled and with a keeper for each. This was in 917 BCE.

Observers believe that Ashoka's empire in India was deeply influenced by Persia and Persian-trained Greek sculptors who were involved in the creation of the extensive lion art that exists in India. According to M.A. Rashid and Reuben David: 'Persian influence in architecture during this time shows Achaemenid influences through the elongated petals and realism in the deeply carved snarling lions and also other animals which are similar to the Persian Persepolis designs, which proves that the lions migrated into India via Persia.'

Some scholars (as do I) doubt the veracity of this argument to account for the presence of lions in the subcontinent. What is apparent, though, is that lion art flourished in areas where lions were never found. Probably the most well-known connection to lions in India is the depiction of the lions on Ashoka's pillars. Romila Thapar and other serious historians argue that the most familiar visual connection with the Ashokan pillar and its lions is found in the region of Persepolis around Susa and Iran. Other scholars like Saryu Doshi believe 'that Egypt inspired Ashoka's conception of the Sarnath pillar bearing the famous lion capital.' Whatever might be the truth about Ashoka's lion pillar, one fact is certain – the lion in it did not come from lions in the natural landscape of India but from connections across the seas. The other fascinating fact of this early art is that there were very few depictions of lions attacking prey or humans; they were always shown in guardian-like postures that appear to be more symbolic than anything else, unlike the depictions of the animal in Assyrian art or even at Persepolis.

It doesn't help matters that, because of royal privilege, anything to do with the lion was always kept a secret and is one of the reasons why there are so many missing links in our understanding of this species.

Every emperor from China to India to Europe and across Persia and more or less everywhere in the known world was in the market for lions. In 1592, a lion and lioness in the Tower menageries in England were even named after King Edward and Queen Elizabeth I. King James in 1622 owned 11 lions. Hunting parks blossomed across Western Europe and even if European royalty didn't manage to shoot that many lions and tigers, they managed to keep themselves busy setting up parks for their animals.

VIKRAM SETH

EXTRACT FROM *FROM HEAVEN LAKE: TRAVELS THROUGH SINKIANG AND TIBET.*

'To buy such things as his beautiful Buddha is . . . to help degrade objects of reverence to assessable and saleable pieces of loot.'

Lhasa

The only foreign mission in Lhasa is the Nepalese Consulate-General, which lies among trees and fields at the western end of the town. It is guarded by a sentry box. Since it is so rarely visited, the sentry is often not in, but is to be found instead strolling, rifle in hand, around the lane beyond the Consulate, with a gait that speaks of unutterable boredom. When I arrive at the gate, he sees me and comes panting back, in time to detain me with fifteen minutes of interrogation. Finally he makes a phone call. I look at the sign above the gate, which reads *Mahavanijya Dootavas* in the Devanagari alphabet. It is vaguely comforting to see the familiar script. The gate opens and a man wearing the conical hat of the Nepalis asks me to enter. Mr Shah, the *Mahavanijyadoot* himself, will be with me shortly.

I sit in the long hall and wait. Pictures of the King and Queen of Nepal stare unnervingly down at me across the low tables and ashtrays and carpets. It is ironic that my first morning in Lhasa should be occupied with planning how best to move on. The Consul-General, Mr Shah, soon appears. He is a striking man: gold teeth, wild black hair and flashing eyes. After a few preliminaries, I say I would like to ask him for his advice on a matter of travel.

'Yes?' he asks, expectantly.

'I've been told that the road and bridge between Tibet and Nepal have been swept away by floods. I didn't hear about this when I was in Beijing. I thought I'd ask you when this happened, and when you think it might be repaired.'

'How did you come to hear of this?'

'Mr Ho, down at the Foreign Affairs Office, mentioned it to me.'

'Well, it's quite true.' Mr Shah pauses. 'They're working on the road on both sides of the border. On the Nepalese side it's motorable until Lamasangu. On the Chinese side it's motorable until Nilamu. I don't know whether in the last few days they've been able to get any further, but I doubt it. It's been raining heavily.' He offers me a cigarette, a Zhonghua, one of China's best brands.

'Have you ever travelled by this road?' I ask.

'Yes, when I came here from Kathmandu about six months ago to take up this post. It's a two-day journey, and the road is good, or, rather, it was. The bridge over the Bhotakoshi at Zhangmu will take a long time to repair: maybe more than year.'

So much, I think, for that route. I go on, a little doubtfully. 'There are no flights between Lhasa and Kathmandu, I suppose?'

'No,' laughs Mr Shah. 'No flights at all.'

'Not even private planes, for instance, for consular officials to get back to Nepal?'

'No. In fact when I return I will have to fly to Chengdu,

then change planes for Kunming, get another plane for Rangoon, another for Calcutta, and a final flight to Kathmandu.' He smiles at the thought. 'I wouldn't advise it,' he continues. 'It takes a week.'

But the alternative is an even longer loop, via Nanjing and Hong Kong. 'I don't know,' I comment. 'Rangoon sounds attractive.'

It is clear that Mr Shah is not taken by Rangoon, but he encourages me nevertheless. 'Yes, well, I hope you enjoy it.' He puffs at his cigarette, going over a few details in his mind. 'You have a Burmese visa?'

'No,' I say uneasily.

'You can only get that in Beijing. You could send your passport in, but that could take weeks.'

Another possibility gone, I think. I may as well give up. Mr Ho was right. I have no choice but to return via Nanjing and Hong Kong. 'So I suppose that's that,' I say. My headache, fitful over the last day, is returning with psychosomatic vengeance.

But Mr Shah muses on. 'Well, when the floods occurred, there *were* some Nepalese citizens trapped on the Chinese side of the border. We asked the Chinese authorities for permission to land a helicopter to evacuate them, but this was refused. Somehow or other, though, and I don't know quite how, they crossed the river and have made it back to Nepal.'

'Yes?' I say, with a small surge of hope.

'Let me draw you a map of what I think they must have done,' says Mr Shah. He draws a north-south line for the Bhotakoshi river, and a few tributaries on both banks. 'The border is somewhat complicated in this area,' he remarks.

'Here, you see, it is marked by the Bhotakoshi itself, but here and here by the tributaries of the river. So there is a northern section where both banks of the Bhotakoshi are in China, a middle section where one is in China, and a southern section where both are in Nepal. The Friendship Bridge at Zhangmu used to be in the middle section, so that when you crossed the bridge you crossed the border at the same time. Do you follow me?'

'Yes,' I say, my eyes on the map.

'Now, after the river rose and swept away the bridge, there is only one way that the Nepalese trapped on this side of the river could have got across.' Mr Shah pauses professorially. His wild hair gives him an almost Einsteinian appearance. 'They must have walked southwards until they found a bridge on the Bhotakoshi which was still intact. Once they crossed the river they could go on to Kathmandu or wherever they wished.' He marks out the route with his finger, which I follow like a mesmerized pigeon.

'Have you thought of *walking* across the border?'

'No.' I am becoming increasingly inarticulate in the face of this possibility. Mr Shah has pleasant voice.

'As I said, the road on the Chinese side is good until Nilamu. From Nilamu to Zhangmu and from there to Lamasangu you'll have to walk – perhaps three or four days on foot, depending on the weather and the state of the forest tracks. If there were a road a truck could do all this in a couple of hours. But it's possible on foot, as long as you get a good guide through the hills. And once you've got to Lamasangu you can take a bus to Kathmandu, and then a flight to Delhi: you might want to think about this.'

I might.

The Consul-General puffs at his cigarette in silence for a minute. 'There is only one problem,' he remarks.

'Oh?'

'Your visa.'

'But I thought I didn't need one for Nepal,' I say, in surprise. 'The Nepalese Embassy in Beijing told me that Indian citizens. . .'

'No, you don't need one, and even if you did I could issue you one here.' Mr Shah looks grave. 'I mean the Chinese exit visa. I don't know if they'll give you special permission to exit through Tibet.'

'How did the Nepalese get permission?'

'They don't need it if they live within a thirty kilometre zone along the border. There's an agreement to that effect.'

'Ah.' I don't know what to say.

'Sometimes they give permission, sometimes they refuse it. When my predecessor was here, two women, an Australian and a Swede, I think, got a lift in his jeep to Kathmandu. But with the bridge down, the Chinese authorities have become more sticky. Two *National Geographic* photographers who flew into Lhasa last month were refused permission to cross into Nepal even though I'd given them Nepalese visas. I don't know what reason was given to them. All I can do is wish you better luck.'

***

I walk over to the Norbulingka Park, deep in thought, but with my headache miraculously cured. The sun is shining, the air is crisp, the sky is blue, and there are ancient trees all around. It is Sunday afternoon, and, just as Gyanseng described it, the park is full of people. To protect themselves from both sun and the sudden afternoon showers, families have stretched large sheets of coloured cloth from tree to tree. They sit on the grass and talk, or watch the scruffy deer in the small zoo, or stroll across to see the Tibetan opera being performed in the open air. The crowd leans forward as a woman kneels and a man reads out a long proclamation. Two warriors fight with stylized bloodthirstiness. Recitative is followed by song and dance. In the various forms of Chinese opera, some of the accompanying instruments are melodic; here, however, there are just drums and gongs. Nearby, two children, unconcerned by the spectacle and noise, are busy stirring a puddle with a stick. I take a photograph of them, and am just about to take another when I hear a voice behind me, in English.

'Hello! Which country are you from?'

'Please don't disturb me,' I say sharply. 'I'm taking photographs.' But it is too late: the children have moved off. Repenting of my rudeness, I turn to speak to the man. He is tall, about twenty-five, dressed in the standard Chinese jacket and baggy trousers, but from his dark skin and sharper features I guess that he is Tibetan. He has friendly eyes, and does not seem to have been offended by my brusqueness. He is nibbling at what looks like a very doughy biscuit.

'India,' I say. 'You are Tibetan?'

'Yes. I am Tibetan.' He speaks carefully, so as not to trip himself up over a grammatical obstacle. 'You have come to Lhasa for what reason?'

'I have come to Lhasa on my way home. I am a student. And you?'

'I live in Lhasa.'

'I mean, what work do you do?'

'I work here in a factory. I learn English in the evenings. Learning English is hard.'

'I think you speak well,' I say mildly.

There is a pause, and I do not know how to go on. These purposeful exchanges in English are all so similar, I think. I look at the biscuit in his hand and realize that I haven't eaten anything since last night's raisins. 'Where can I buy some biscuits?' I ask. 'Is there a shop nearby?'

'Come with me, please. You will meet my family.' With a pleasant mixture of formality and assertiveness Norbu ignores my splutterings and leads me to where about twenty people – more a clan than a family – are sitting on the ground below a cloth canopy: aunts, uncles, cousins, nephews, nieces. Their voices rise and fall in a joyful babble. His father is gambling with friends in a corner. Children are yelling above the hubbub. Norbu introduces his girlfriend, who is very shy. She offers me a bowl of yak-butter tea.

The only common language for the three of us is Chinese, and Norbu speaks it beautifully, despite the fact that he has never been outside Tibet. His father, who was in India many years ago, interrupts his game for a few minutes to talk about Darjeeling in the 1930s, the music of Sahgal, and, when I ask him a direct question, about changes in Tibet – though in terms of cautious generality. He, like his son, is a tall and well-built man, but there is a curious frailness to him,

'As if some dire constraint of pain, or rage
Of sickness felt by him in times long past
A more than human weight upon his frame had cast.'

But gossiping and gambling with his friends, he seems happy enough. He drinks *chang* (*qingke* wine) from a silver bowl, and I am given a bowl too. It tastes like a dry white wine, enjoyable though not overpoweringly potent. Huge tins of sweet and savoury biscuits and home-made snacks are passed around, and everyone in turn is made to sing a song (I dust off the perennial favourite, 'Awara'). Even the shyest little girl sings with great gusto. When I leave I am filled with their contagious happiness. It is some days before I become aware of the harsh backdrop against which this lighthearted scene has been played.

***

Bath hour is not yet over in the Number One Guest House; a steaming hot shower rids me of the dust and dirt of the journey. The soapy water pours off my hair in a black stream, and the warmth feels exquisite to my fatigued and neglected body. Downstairs, I meet a group of Italians who are here on a 'Tibet Safari'. They are quite young as far as tour groups go – about fortyish – and very lively, through unfortunately constrained by the programme organized by their Tourist Office guides. We drink lemon and orange juice which they have prepared from packets of powder. I am intoxicated by the sound of their names – Addilio, Ettore, Gigi, Emilio, Marina, Igea. . .

Ettore and I, who can communicate only through gestures and pidgin German, go to the Jokhang temple the next day. This temple, located in the centre of the old town, in the middle of an octagonal circuit of streets, is one of the holiest centres of Tibetan Buddhism, and, with its gold roof sloping elegantly above the busy street, one of the most beautiful. The buildings around it are typically Tibetan, of white stone: there are shops and dwellings on the first floor, deep narrow cells whose interiors can only be dimly glimpsed. At the temple itself we are stopped by a 'responsible person' and spend three-quarters of an hour trying to get in, persuading and protesting by turns. Three ultra-bureaucratic and mendacious unit-leaders – for this temple, too, is a 'unit' – haul us to the office and growl aggressively on, Cerberus-like, about regulations and foreigners and introductory letters. (When I go to the Potala I will make sure I shed all signs of foreignness.) When I counter one argument, they switch to another: there are no monks 'on duty', the keys are not available. Eventually I get through to Mr Ho on the phone, and he solves the problem, suggesting at the same time that I be calmer in my approach to things. Upon payment of 10 yuan we are allowed to go in. (For 150 yuan people are permitted to take photographs in the rooms.)

We see the magnificent inner hall of the temple, with niches and alcoves in the sides, silk hangings, fragrant yak-butter lamps. Murals in reds and greens give life to the walls, and within the halls are gold Buddhas, each with a different expression or posture or gesture; future and past Buddhas, Guanyins and Sakyamunis; Buddhas compassionate and Buddhas calm. The most important Sakyamuni is protected behind a heavy chain-meshed entrance.

The Jokhang Temple (I learn from the introduction to a set of postcards) was built by the Tibetan King Songtsan Gambo in the middle of the seventh century, and has been damaged and repaired several times through the centuries. In 1961 the temple was listed by the State Council of the People's Republic as an ancient monument selected for special protection, but it nevertheless suffered heavy damage during the Cultural Revolution. It has been restored since then. What a tragedy that such beauty should still be so unpleasantly inaccessible.

King Songtsan Gambo (who is also said to have founded the Potala) is credited with introducing Buddhism into Tibet, having reputedly been converted by his Chinese and Nepalese wives, both Buddhists. While the monarchy died out a few generations later, Buddhism went on growing and gradually replaced Bön, the former shamanistic religion of the area. By the eleventh century it appears that secular power was also in the hands of a number of Buddhist communities.

Many of the earliest Indian gurus who came to preach in Tibet were greatly influenced by Tantric Hinduism; some of the first classics to be translated into Tibetan were consequently Tantric texts. This undercurrent of Tantrism, together with survivals from Bön shamanism, give the Buddhism of Tibet much of its unique flavour.

One figure, the great Tsongkapa (died 1410) stands out in the history of Tibetan Buddhism. He reformed and consolidated the practice of the religion so comprehensively that there is hardly an institution that does not bear his imprint. The 'yellow hat' or 'reformed' sect (which became the established sect in Tibet); the three monasteries near Lhasa – Ganden, Drepung and Sera; the system of rule and ritual for monks and initiates; all these were founded during his life under his direction, or else soon after his death. In addition to this he was a renowned teacher of esoteric Buddhism, which is communicated not through texts but directly from teacher to disciple.

The spiritual leadership passed on after Tsongkapa to a series of high lamas. Later, with the help of the Mongolian princes (Mongolia had meanwhile been converted to Buddhism), secular power was concentrated in the hands of the Dalai Lama, whose seat was Lhasa. The Panchen Lama, whose seat was the Zashilumpo monastery in Shigatse, had no secular power but a spiritual position second only to the Dalai Lama. In time high lamas themselves began to be worshipped, both in life and after death; a complex pantheon of Buddhas, Bodhisattvas and Lamas can be seen in all the great temples and monasteries of Tibetan Buddhism even today.

***

In the outer court of the Jokhang, facing the street, worshippers are grinding flour, spinning prayer-wheels, chanting incantations. The air is filled with the scent of herbs and dust. Two men are circling the temple, prostrating themselves, marking with a stone the spot that their heads touch, rising, moving to the spot marked, and then prostrating themselves again. Like spinning the prayer-wheel, this is a way of accumulating merit. For some reason the crowd of people gathered around them cheers one and jeers the other.

Opposite the Jokhang stands a withered tree, more than a thousand years old, brought by a Tang princess from China when she married King Songtsan Gambo; pilgrims from all over Tibet are camped below it in yak-hide tents, together with a number of smiling and grubby children with matted hair. I move around the octagonal street clockwise like everyone else (except army jeeps and a sample of variously-sized belligerent dogs). I am followed by a troop of leech-like hawkers selling pieces of jade, turquoise earrings, daggers, old Tibetan religious objects and ornaments and silver coins. Women sell yak yogurt in plump glass jars at corners; also joints of yak meat, pieces of yak bone, tomatoes, spring onions and a dark hard cheese-like substance that I buy, to my almost immediate regret. A crisp cucumber helps me to forget the strange taste.

The Han population of Lhasa is now greater that the Tibetan population, but this part of the old town is almost exclusively Tibetan. Ever here, near the Jokhang, the blue jackets and trousers are common, but it is the varied clothing of the Tibetans that catches the eye. The tall pilgrims from Chamdo are the most striking: red string intertwined with their hair, daggers hanging from their belts, they have a fierceness of facial expression well-suited to their martial bearing. A woman from Qinghai has her hair plaited in a complex ornamental panel behind her, which reaches almost to her waist, and three strips of banded cloth fall like an apron in front of her dress. She emerges from a tent, pulling a wailing child behind her. Four small boys catch sight of my camera; their faces caked in grime and snot, healthy in their ragged clothes, they run after me begging for money. An old woman sits behind a wooden table covered with brightly striped cotton, cutting off prayer-flags from a long bolt of cloth. She is also selling silver ornaments, religious objects, plastic combs, hair curlers, small locks, cloth shoes, yak leather boots, inner soles, lacquer cups, postcards, two or three books and a large frayed orange carpet with a dragon design. A man wearing a green felt bowler hat lures me into the back of a shop and attempts to sell me a dagger. I am not interested. Its scabbard is encrusted with semiprecious stones. I am still not interested. Am I interested in a thirty centimetres high Buddha statuette? It is, he tells me repeatedly, very beautiful. It comes from a temple, but the man is unwilling to say how he came by it. No, I am not interested. Will I at least look at it? No. it is only on the sixth refusal that he releases my arm.

My arm is next grabbed by a couple carrying a silver prayer-wheel. Murmuring '*kuchi-kuchi-kuchi*', they point at my camera. I try to show them that this is not a Polaroid, but they are adamant. When I snap a couple of shots, they demand money. I refuse; they move away without, surprisingly, any sign of ill-will. As I walk away from the octagon in the direction of the guest house, the green bowler makes yet another venal overture. I tell him to leave me alone. To buy such things as his beautiful Buddha is to encourage further plunder of the temples and to help degrade objects of reverence to assessable and saleable pieces of loot.

***

The sun is strong by ten in the morning, when I walk over to Mr Ho's office to tell him I'm thinking of walking to

Nepal. Mr Ho is flustered. His baby son is playing outside, picking up handfuls of gravel and gurgling. He offers his son a boiled sweet to distract him – Chinese parents often resort to boiled sweets – and tells me that the police want to interview me. When would be best? Tomorrow morning? The sooner the better, I say. I ask him to mention my plans so that they can at the same time ask me whatever questions they want to about my onward journey. Time is running out. The few days left on my travel pass and residence permit are one by one trickling away.

In a department store, distressingly similar to those in other cities of China (except, perhaps, that AA batteries are even less available here), my eyes fall on a toy bear with a camera. The bear moves: its head nods, it lifts its camera to eye-level, and a light flashes. On impulse I buy the bizarre beast for Mr Ho's little boy. But as I leave the store I begin to wonder whether I should have bought it. If I give it to Mr Ho now he may consider it an improper gift as my case is under consideration. If I give it to him after I have got my special exit endorsement, it may be seen as a reward, again improper. It occurs to me that the only appropriate circumstance in which I can give it is if I don't get permission to exit through Tibet.

With this depressing speculation in mind, I enter the guest house to hear that the Public Security Bureau has sent some people around. I am first examined in a general way by an officer called Zhao, clad in the immaculately clean and pressed white jacket and trousers of the police. Her questions, it seems to me, are intended as a check of my bona fides. In a fog of relevant and irrelevant details, she presses me again and again on crucial points – my status, my purpose in coming to Tibet – asking me, in a comprehensive but circumlocutory way, to explain everything that could be construed as an inconsistency. Five minutes after she has left, two other officers enter, a Long and a Liu. They have with them the sheet of paper on which Zhao took notes. At first they go over the same ground. I pull out letters and testimonials and certificates and research forms, anything that is printed or might look official, again regardless of relevance. When they ask about my proposed route to Nepal, I bring out the map that Mr Shah has drawn. I also enquire about the possibility of going directly to India via the road through Yadong. This idea is immediately rejected.

The officers are totally non-committal about whether or not I will get permission to exit from Tibet. The matter has to be decided 'in consultation', but with whom I cannot discover. I mention that unless I am out of Lhasa when my Chinese residence permit expires at the end of the month, it will be their duty to arrest me. They laugh politely.

By this time Mr Shah (who has invited me for dinner) has arrived at the guest house to give me a lift. He sits in a long black car with a long black cigarette holder in his mouth. The officers peep out of the window and are suddenly apologetic. They suggest that we continue the interrogation later; but I want to get it over with once and for all. When, ten minutes later, they leave, they take with them my passport and travel pass: I feel a little naked without them. I ask the police when I should contact them again; they tell me that they will get in touch with me. I ask them when that might be. 'When we have come to a decision,' they reply. 'Things take time.'

At the Consulate-General, over Haig on and off the rocks and *lassi* (made from yak yogurt – the first *lassi* I've had in years), Mr Shah and I reminisce about Patna. I lived there for ten long years. Mr Shah was there for only two – he studied international relations at the university – but he feels a greater attachment to Patna than to Delhi, where he has worked for much longer. 'Ah,' he says, dandling his daughter on his lap, 'when I flew over Patna the last time, I pointed out the Golghar granary to my wife – and the red-bricked Darbhanga House, where I lived as a student; I made lifelong friends there, and got addicted to Charminar cigarettes. In 1955 they used to cost two annas for a pack of ten.' We do not speak in English today, and when Mr Shah says he is surprised that I haven't lost all my Hindi after living abroad for so many years, I am absurdly pleased. When he offers to send information about my safe arrival in Lhasa to my family (by radio relay), I am ecstatic. My message – 'DEAR MAMA PAPA SHANTUM AND ARADHANA I HAVE ARRIVED IN LHASA AND WILL BE IN KATHMANDU IN A FEW DAYS DO NOT WORRY ABOUT ME LOTS OF LOVE VIKRAM' – is perhaps over-optimistic, but I have downed a good deal of Mr Shah's Scotch by this time.

Next morning I walk across People's Street to buy a map of Lhasa at the bookstore. Inside, between 'literature' and 'technology', is an altar to Mao: a white bust of the Great Helmsman, surrounded by a low semi-circular wall of his maroon-bound books, with flower vases at each end. Huge red quotations from his works hang on the walls. As I stare at this shrine (the remnant of a past age; one no longer sees such monstrosities in the rest of China), I feel a sudden weakness in my legs and almost collapse, so that I have to support myself against a counter. The shop assistants are alarmed at what must look like an overpowering spiritual revelation. They offer to escort me back to the guest house. I am all right, I insist. The guest house is just across the street.

But I am not all right. I have barely got back to my room when I collapse on the bed. All the old symptoms of headache, nausea and shortness of breath are back, together with an attack of diarrhoea for good measure. I have over-exerted myself, and have drunk too much alcohol; both unwise at this altitude. I order myself to spend a day in bed, and to suppress all exploratory instincts.

I spend the day writing postcards: this seems a surreal activity in Lhasa, but then the guest house attendants are playing frisbee outside my window and whistling 'Santa Lucia'. I look over a book I bought in Dunhuang: *Everyday Language for Hotel Personnel – 1000 English Sentences.* Tourism is now a big thing in China: new five-star hotels are going up in several cities, under collaboration contracts with foreign firms. The book includes sentences like 'I want to have a manicure,' and 'Please curl the hair on the temples towards the front, curl the hair on the sides outwards, and make the hair on top higher.' 'There are some cockroaches in this room; please clear them out immediately.' 'It is a misunderstanding, I am afraid. The Chinese people and the Japanese people are very friendly towards each other.' On that cheerful note I close that book and open my *Lao Tzu.*

ZAI WHITAKER

EXTRACT FROM *COBRA IN MY KITCHEN: STORIES, POEMS AND PIECES.*

'When a cobra spreads its hood and sits up, hissing, it's nothing but bluff and pretence. It wants you to think it is much more dangerous than it really is.'

Leave Your Tail and Run!
(How Reptiles Defend Themselves)

It's probably not much fun being a small reptile – snake, lizard, crocodile, turtle or tortoise. Because you always have to be alert for predators. A young crocodile, for example, can be gobbled up by birds, jackals, frogs, big fish, big crocodiles, turtles, man . . . to name a few. Not much time to relax, and a lot of worries. How can a small animal defend itself against a much, much larger predator? It would be ridiculous for a tree snake to pretend it could fight off an eagle, or for a skink to believe it could overpower a crocodile. So the next best thing is to bluff and trick your way through life, and reptiles are very good at this.

When a cobra spreads its hood and sits up, hissing, it's nothing but bluff and pretence. It wants you to think it is much more dangerous than it really is. Frogs bloat their bodies with air to make themselves look big and scary. Snakes and lizards open their mouths wide and puff themselves up. Quite often, this is enough to frighten away the bird or other predator that is looking for food.

Crocodiles and lizards also do a 'high walk', raising their bodies off the ground to look scary. It is rather funny to see a small gecko raising itself in this boastful posture. But it works, and another creature that is trying to invade its territory – or eat it up – will quickly retreat.

Some lizards, like geckos and skinks, can drop their tails when caught. This is a very useful trick. It directs the attention of the predator away from the head of the animal, to the tail . . . without which it can manage until it grows back. While the predator is puzzling over the wriggling item, the animal runs off.

Soon, another tail will grow. How is it possible to drop a tail? The muscles of the vertebrae of these animals are so loosely connected that they separate, and break off, easily. The broken part wriggles for a while because it retains its muscular activity for some time after coming off. Geckos can chuck their tails off even before they are caught! This is indeed useful. While the predator is scratching its head in wonder – or chomping on the tail – the gecko's off. However, at certain times of year, when food is scarce, they are not so happy about dropping their tail, because that's where fat is stored.

The stout sand boa, when attacked by a mongoose or bird of prey, tucks its head under its coils and waves its tail in the air. The head and tail of this snake look very similar. The idea is to fool the predator into attacking the tail rather than the head. Sand boas often have scarred and injured tails, showing that this trick works. The spiny-tailed lizard of north-western India has a rough, horny tail which is used as a defence against snakes. Snakes are the main predators of this lizard. When it hears a snake approaching its burrow, the lizard sticks its tail out and attacks the snake by shaking it violently. The meat of the spiny-tailed lizard is eaten by some local tribes. To catch it, they make a rustling, snaky sound with a broom outside the hole and when the tail comes out, they grab it and pull out the lizard.

Others, like the ringhals of south Africa and the American hog-nosed snake, roll over and play dead, while the trinket snake freezes in position for minutes on end, hoping to escape detection.

Ever heard a Russell's viper hiss? It sounds like a steam engine. The hissing of snakes is rather discouraging, and makes you want to be far away. Crocodiles, and even turtles, also hiss, growl, groan and moan in an effort to frighten predators. The deep, throaty growl of the king cobra and rat snake is a sound to remember. The rattlesnakes of the United States face the enemy and shake their rattle, which is loud enough to be heard thirty metres away. People often ask why venomous snakes need to hiss, and puff, and bluff, when their venom can easily kill most of their enemies. But the snake doesn't know this! Snake venom is a type of saliva which helps it to kill and digest prey. When a snake bites a foot that has accidentally stepped on it, it doesn't know that the bite will lead to a miserable time in hospital, or even death.

One of the best defences is speed. Many reptiles can move fast. A saltwater crocodile, believe it or not, can actually gallop like a horse! Some species of snakes and lizards can disappear in a flash. The poor old turtle is at a disadvantage, but its hard shell is good protection. And, come to think of it, moving very, very slowly – like the chameleon does – can be helpful too. By moving slowly, you can go unnoticed, as well as get away from the danger zone.

Another way to avoid being attacked and eaten is to hide and hope for the best. In this, camouflage is very useful. This means that the animal has the same colouring as its surroundings. A green vine snake gets lost among leaves, and the mud-coloured sand boa just becomes part of the earth. Lying on the banks of rivers, crocodiles look like rocks, until they are disturbed . . . and then – splash! Often, a harmless little animal mimics, or copies, another more dangerous animal to fool predators. The bright red tails and fast movement of skinks are very centipede-like.

The larger reptiles of course have a much easier time. They have few predators and little to fear. No animal is going to mess with a large crocodile, or anaconda, or python . . . except man. But in their jungle homes they are master predators who can take life easy. They can cruise along the river or lie lazily in the sun without having to worry about a sudden attack. They are the lucky ones.

Notes

From an Undelivered Speech, 1936: Bhimrao Ramji Ambedkar

1. Ambedkar is referring to the socialists within the Congress who in 1934 formed a faction called the Congress Socialist Party (CSP). Jawaharlal Nehru, at this juncture, was also actively advocating socialist ideas but did join the CSP.
2. Comitia Centuriata, or the Century Assembly, was originally an assembly of the Roman military, but soon turned into a political assembly, and became one of the three public assemblies of the Republic of Rome where citizens, grouped into 'centuries', voted on legislative, electoral and judicial matters. In the early days, entry to the Senate was only by birth and rank – so the patricians called the shots. Even in the Comitia Centuriata, instituted in about 450 BCE, entry was restricted initially to the patricians and the plebeians were kept at bay. Even after the Comitia Centuriata came to include plebeians, its organization and voting system nevertheless gave greater influence to the rich than to the poor, which as Ambedkar points out, resembled the Communal Award. Ambedkar understands, in the caste context, the plight of plebeians with voting rights as being similar to that of the Untouchables who were denied a separate electorate – the mere right to vote does not necessarily empower them. For more on the evolution of the Roman republic, see Olga Tellegen-Couperus (1993). [Tellegen-Couperus, Olga. 1993. *A Short History of Roman Law*. London: Routledge.]
3. While Delphi, associated with the Greek god Apollo, was an important site in Hellenic political life, the Romans did not seem to consult the Oracle regularly owing to its considerable distance from Rome. They, however, tended to refer to the Sibylline Books, kept at the Capitolium. See Fontenrose (1978). For an account of the hold of religion on the Romans, see Rupke (2007). [Fontenrose, Joseph. 1978. *The Delphic Oracle: Its Responses and Operations, with a Catalogue of Responses*. Berkeley, University of California Press; Rupke, Jörg, ed. 2007. *A Companion to Roman Religion*. Oxford: Blackwell.]
4. Ambedkar's ire here is likely directed at the socialist turn within the Congress. Following the 1936 Congress session in Lucknow,

where Nehru took over as party president at Gandhi's behest, the Agrarian Resolution declared that 'the most important and urgent problem of the country is the appalling poverty, unemployment and indebtedness of the peasantry, fundamentally due to the antiquated and repressive land revenue system'. Nehru and the few socialists he managed to sneak into the thirteen-member Congress Working committee (CWC) – Acharya Narayan Dev, Jayaprakash Narayan and Achyut Patwardhan – sought to end the 'middle class domination' of the Congress and sought direct representation for peasants and workers in the party. But tacitly backed by Gandhi, the right wing within the Congress opposed Nehru's socialist tendencies. On 29 June 1936, CWC members Babu Rajendra Prasad, Jairamdas Daulatram, Jamnalal Bajaj, Acharya Kriplalani and S.D. Dev submitted their resignations from the CWC in a joint letter, contending that Nehru's preaching of socialism in his election speeches was 'prejudicial to the interests of the country and to the success of the national struggle for freedom'. Gandhi backed the conservatives, as did the business classes. Subsequently Nehru recanted. For a detailed account of Nehru and socialism, see R.C. Dutt (1980,30–90). [Dutt, R.C. 1980. *Socialism of Jawaharlal Nehru*. New Delhi: Abhinav.]

5. Ambedkar (in Das, 2010b,49–68) mounts a more direct attack on the socialists in the presidential address delivered on 12 and 13 February, 1938, to the GIP (Great Indian Peninsular) Railway Depressed Classes Workmen's Conference held in Nashik, Manmad district. In this speech he offers a trenchant critique of capitalism and Brahmanism, and examines the problems with Indian socialists at greater length. Ambedkar was addressing the GIP conference in his capacity as president of the Independent Labour Party, the first political party founded by him in August 1936, a few months after the publication of *Annihilation of Caste*. [Das, Bhagwan. 2010a. *In Pursuit of Ambedkar: A Memoir*. New Delhi: Navayana.]
6. Emphasis in original.
7. Ambedkar is echoing the words of Dewey. According to Mukherjee (2009,347): 'So deeply embedded is Dewey's thought in Ambedkar's consciousness that quite often his words flow through Ambedkar's discourse without quotation marks.' She also notes 'how Ambedkar culled sentences from *Democracy and Education* to describe his version of the ideal society' (351). Ambedkar expresses his debt to Dewey in section 25.4 of AoC. The relevant paragraph from Dewey's *Democracy and Education*, quoted by Mukherjee, reads: 'A democratic criterion requires us to develop capacity to the point

of competency to choose and make its own career. This principle is violated when the attempt is made to fit individuals in advance for definite industrial callings, selected not on the basis of trained original capacities, but on that of the wealth or social status of parents' (364). See Dewey (1961). All further citations from *Democracy and Education* are from the online edition. [Mukherjee, Arun P. 2009. "B.R. Ambedkar, John Dewey, and the Meaning of Democracy." New Literary History 40 (2): 345–70; Dewey, John. 1916. *Democracy and Education: An Introduction to the Philosophy of Education.* Repr. New York: Macmillan, 1958. Indian ed. Aakar Books. New Delhi 2004. Available online: Electronic Text Center, University of Virhginia Library: http://etext.lib.virginia.edu/toc/modeng/public/DewDemo.html.Accessed 15 March 2013.]

8. John Dewey was an advocate of industrial democracy, which, in Noam Chomsky's (2003) words 'means democratizing production, commerce, and so on, which means eliminating the whole structure of capitalist hierarchy'. Chomsky terms Dewey a 'radical' in this interview. In another essay, Chomsky (2013) says: 'Dewey called for workers to be "masters of their own industrial fate" and for all institutions to be brought under public control, including the means of production, exchange, publicity, transportation and communication. Short of this, Dewey argued, politics will remain "the shadow cast on society by big business."' [Chomsky, Noam. 2003. On Dewey. http://www.american-philosophy.org/Chomsky_on_Dewey_transcript_2003.html.]
9. Ethnology draws upon ethnographic material to compare and contrast different cultures. Ethnography is the study of single groups through direct contact with their cultures. In the nineteenth century, ethnologists and ethnographers studied caste mainly as a subsidiary exercise in the supposedly higher and grander task of uncovering the evolutionary heritage of all humanity. In doing so they contributed to the 'Orientalist' exercise of the census and gazetteers and to the racial understanding of caste. Caste was thus subsumed into theories of biologically determined race essences. Ambedkar, in fact, begins his 1916 essay, 'Castes in India', with a reference to ethnology. Further, on caste and ethnology, see Bayly (1999,11–19); and Dirks (2001,126–38). See also Ketkar (1909/1998,165–70). [Bayly, Susan. 1999. *Caste, Society and Politics in India: from the Eighteenth Century to Modern India.* Cambridge: Cambridge University Press; Dirks, Nicholas B. 2001. *Castes of Mind: Colonialism and the Making of Modern India.* New

Delhi: Permanent Black; Ketkar, S.V. 1998. *History of Caste in India*. New Delhi: Low Price Publications. (Orig. publ. 1909.]

10. Devadatta Ramakrishna Bhandarkar (1875–1950) was an epigraphist and archaeologist who worked for the Archaeological Survey of India. Ambedkar is citing from p.37 of this 1911 essay. Based on epigraphic research, Bhandakar uses evidence from the Vedas and the epics of the Hindu tradition, such as the *Rig Veda* and the Mahabharata, to disprove the 'purity of blood' myth attributed to Brahmins. 'It may be said that after all the Mahabharata ... is a conglomeration of legends, which are not of much historical importance, though they cannot be objected to by an orthodox Brahmana and consequently may be adduced to silence his pretensions to purity of origin and the consequent highest place in Hindu society' (1911,10). [Bhandarkar, D.R. 1911. "Foreign Elements in the Hindu Population." *Indian Antiquary* 40: 7–37.]
11. In his understanding of the caste system and its evolution, Ambedkar here differs strongly from Brahminic appropriations (such as by B.G. Tilak who authored the *Arctic Home in the Vedas*, 1903) of the racial theory of Aryans and Dravidians propounded by European Indologists. In fact, as seen in (Arundhati) Roy's introduction to this edition, even Gandhi, in his South Africa years, strongly believed in the British and India's ruling classes both being 'Aryan'. Ambedkar, however, also differs on this front from his predecessor and radical thinker Jotiba Phule and his contemporary fellow-traveller 'Periyar' E.V. Ramasamy Naicker (1879–1973) who turned the racial theory inside out, postulated a pre-Aryan golden age, and regarded the Brahmins as Aryans, and hence foreigners, who imposed the caste system upon the non-Brahmins who were seen as an indigenous race. For Phule's writings, especially Gulamgiri (Slavery, 1873), see G.P. Deshpande (2002,23–101). Periyar, on the eve of independence, quite radically called upon the Dravidian people of South India to 'guard against the transfer of power from the British to the Aryans' (*The Hindu*, 11 February 1946). As sociologist T.K. Oommen (2005,99) argues, 'According to Periyar, Brahmins had tried to foist their language and social system on Dravidians to erase their race consciousness and, therefore, he constantly reminded the Dravidians to uphold their "race consciousness". However, Periyar did not advocate the superiority of one race over the other but insisted on [the] equality of all races. Thus the fundamental difference between Aryan Hinduism and Dravidian Hinduism is crucial: the former [is] hegemonic, but the latter is emancipatory.' [Tilak, B.G. 1903. *The*

Arctic Home in the Vedas: Being also the New Key to the Interpretation of Many Vedic Texts and Legends. Pune: Tilak Bros.; Deshpande, G.P., ed. 2002. Selected Writings of Jotirao Phule. New Delhi: LeftWord; Oommen, T.K. 2005. Crisis and Contention in Indian Society. New Delhi: Sage.]

Kunwar Singh: Jim Corbett

1. The *runi* tree against which the tigress – who evidently had just given birth to cubs in that area, and who resented the presence of human beings – pinned Har Singh was about 18 inches thick, and in her rage the tigress tore away a third of it. This tree became a landmark for all who shot or poached in the Garuppu jungles until, some 25 years later, it was destroyed by a forest fire.

   Har Singh, in spite of the rough and ready treatment he received at the hands of his three friends, and in spite of the vegetation that went inside him, suffered no ill effects from his wound, and lived to die of old age.

S Is for Schools: Nandan Nilekani

1. Balachandra Rajan, *Under Western Eyes: India from Milton to Macaulay*, Duke University Press, 1999.
2. Ibid.
3. Krishna Kumar, *Political Agenda of Education*, Sage Publications, 2005.
4. Ibid.
5. Ibid.
6. Ibid.
7. Poromesh Acharya, 'Education, Politics and Social structure', in *Education and Process of Change*, edited by R. Ghosh and M. Zachariah, Sage Publications, 1987.
8. Constituent Assembly of India, Vol. 7, 23 November 1954.
9. Poromesh Acharya, 'Education, Politics and Social structure', in *Education and Process of Change*, edited by R. Ghosh and M. Zachariah, Sage Publications, 1987.
10. V.S. Naipaul, *India: A Wounded Civilization*, Penguin Books Ltd, 1979.
11. Amit Varma, 'Fund Schooling, Not Schools'. *Mint*, 20 September 2007.

Contributors

1. A.P.J. Kalam

Dr Avul Pakir Jainulabdeen Abdul Kalam (1931–2015) was a leading scientist whose extensive work spread across the domains of defence, nuclear and aerospace departments, among others. This 'Missile Man of India' served as the president of India from 2002 to 2007. In addition to being the recipient of India's highest civilian honour, the Bharat Ratna, Dr Kalam was known for cultivating the imagination of young people through personal interactions and his books.

2. Bhagat Singh

Bhagat Singh (1907–23) was an eminent revolutionary figure in India's fight for independence. Born into a Sikh family, he gradually got influenced by both anarchism and Marxism. To avenge the murder of Lala Lajpat Rai, he participated in an attack on a British police officer and later also became involved in bombing the Central Legislative Assembly while shouting slogans and throwing pamphlets. This martyr's life, which ended at only twenty-three, has been portrayed in several plays and movies.

3. Bhimrao Ramji Ambedkar

Dr B.R. Ambedkar (1891–1956) was the first law minister of independent India. Popularly known as Babasaheb, he was the chief architect of the drafting of the Constitution of India. After completing his studies, he directed his life towards political activities, striving to attain social justice in matters of both caste and gender. He was posthumously awarded the Bharat Ratna in 1990.

4. Dilip Salwi

Dilip Salwi (1952–2004) was a sci-fi author with more than 30 books. Known as the 'Indian Asimov', he was recognized and acclaimed for his contribution in advancing science, particularly among children. He received the NCERT National Award for his collection of short stories *The Robots Are Coming*. He has been associated with both fictional and non-fictional works.

5. Jawaharlal Nehru

Pandit Jawaharlal Nehru (1889–1964) was the first prime minister and external affairs minister of independent India. One of the most prominent figures of India's freedom movement, along with Mahatma Gandhi, he helped shape India's transformation into a democratic republic. In India, Chacha Nehru's birthday on 14 November is celebrated as Children's Day for his contribution towards promoting education. He also wrote several books and was awarded the Bharat Ratna in 1955.

6. Jayant V. Narlikar

Dr Jayant Vishnu Narlikar (1938–) is a pioneering astrophysicist. Several prestigious awards have been conferred on him, such as the Padma Vibushan, the Padma Bhushan, and the Kalinga Award by UNESCO for his widespread research and propagation of science. Apart from being associated with the NCERT as a consultant for textbooks, he has also written many books and was given the Sahitya Akademi Award for his autobiography in 2014.

7. Jim Corbett

Edward James 'Jim' Corbett (1875–1955) was a colonel in the British Indian Army, and famous for hunting and killing man-eating jungle cats. This Anglo-Indian hunter turned conservationist and helped in establishing a national park for the protection of tigers, which is now famously known as the Jim Corbett National Park. He authored many books based on his experiences as a naturalist.

8. Leila Seth

Born in Lucknow, Leila Seth (1930–) was the first woman to be appointed as judge on the Delhi High Court in 1978. She went on to become the first female Chief Justice of a State (Himachal Pradesh) High Court, in 1991. She also served on the Law Commission of India. Novelist and poet Vikram Seth's mother, Leila Seth penned her autobiography in 2003.

9. Mohandas Karamchand Gandhi

Mahatma Gandhi (1869–1948) was the most prominent freedom fighter during India's struggle for sovereignty. Popularly known as Bapu (the 'father of the nation'), he emphasized ahimsa and civil disobedience to achieve liberty. He strove to eradicate untouchability and professed Swaraj or self-rule. He wrote profusely on several topics and his birthday on 2 October is observed as the International Day of Non-violence.

10. Nandan Nilekani

Nandan Nilekani (1955–) is the co-founder of Infosys, an Indian multinational company. He later gave up co-chairmanship of the company in order to become the chairman in the governmental agency of the Unique Identification Authority of India (UIDAI). *Time* magazine recognized him as one of the 100 most influential people in the world twice, in 2006 and 2009. He was awarded the Padma Bhushan in 2006.

11. Rabindranath Tagore

Rabindranath Tagore (1861–1941) was an eclectic artist whose craft in the fields of music, painting, theatre and literature forms a significant part of Bengali as well as Indian arts history. He was the first non-European to win the Nobel Prize for Literature in 1913, largely for his collection of poems, *Gitanjali*. His two musical pieces, namely *Jana Gana Mana* and *Amar Sonar Bangla*, are the national anthems of India and Bangladesh respectively. He also founded Visva-Bharati University, which boasts of a highly distinguished alumni list.

12. Ruskin Bond

Ruskin Bond (1934–) is a writer who lives in Landour, Mussoorie, Uttarakhand. His first novel, *The Room on the Roof*, written at the young age of seventeen, won the John Llewellyn Rhys Prize. Many of his works have been shaped by his personal experiences and he has been lauded particularly for his writing for children. He has also received many prestigious awards, such as the Sahitya Akademi Award, the Padma Shri and the Padma Bhushan.

13. Sarojini Naidu

Sarojini Naidu (1879–1949) was a leading freedom fighter who became the first Indian woman to become the president of the Indian National Congress. She was also the first female governor of an independent Indian state. Popularly known as The Nightingale of India, this skilled orator was also a distinguished poet.

14. Sarvepalli Radhakrishnan

Dr S. Radhakrishnan (1888–1975) was the first vice president and the second president of independent India. He was a profound scholar with intensive work in the fields of philosophy and religion. He was awarded the Bharat Ratna in 1954. His birthday on 5 September is celebrated as Teacher's Day in honour of his saying that 'teachers should be the best minds in the country'.

15. Sheila Dhar

Sheila Dhar (1929–2001) was a Hindustani classical singer and a skilled weaver of tales in which she often expounded on her musical propensities, and the art of singing and other singers. She taught English literature at Delhi University for a while. Her works, songs and books encompass a cultural terrain that caters to all age groups.

16. Subhas Chandra Bose

S.C. Bose (1897–1945) was a prominent nationalist, known for his declaration of Purna Swaraj and encouragement of militant and armed resistance. Also known by the sobriquet Netaji, he is appreciated for his patriotism, but his associations with fascist powers such as Hitler-led Nazi Germany and Japan have made him a conflicted figure. His death ascribed to a plane crash in 1945 has remained a source of speculation till date.

17. Subroto Bagchi

Subroto Bagchi (1957–) is the co-founder and chairman of Mindtree, a multinational IT company designed to assist businesses to prosper. This leading visionary is also a bestselling author of works such as *The High Performance Entrepreneur, Go Kiss the World* and *The Elephant Catchers.* He is also involved with social issues.

18. Sudha Murty

Sudha Murty (1950–) is a prolific fiction writer and a children's writer, both in Kannada and English, and has been the recipient of awards such as the R.K. Narayan Award for Literature and the Padma Shri. She is also the chairperson of the Infosys Foundation, a non-profit body with the aim to support the underprivileged classes. She is a vigorous social activist, supporting diverse issues such as women empowerment, education, public hygiene, art and culture.

19. Swami Vivekananda

Born Narendranath Dutta (1863–1902), he took up monastic vows and adopted the name 'Vivekananda'. He was one of the most influential figures in the revival of Vedanta philosophy and in bridging the cultural gap between the Indian subcontinent and the western world. On September 11, 1893, he delivered his remarkable speech on the need for harmony between religions in Chicago and this day is now recognized as World Brotherhood Day. He wrote many spiritual works. His birthday on 12 January is celebrated as National Youth Day in India.

20. Valmik Thapar

Valmik Thapar (1952–), a naturalist and conservationist, is the founder of the wildlife NGO, Ranthambore Foundation. This wildlife expert has written many books and produced several documentaries. Most notably, he has presented *Land of the Tiger*, a BBC nature documentary series showcasing India's flora and fauna in its scenic landscape. He has also been a member of several government panels concerned with the preservation of nature.

21. Vikram Seth

Vikram Seth (1952–) is a writer whose ouevre includes poems, novels, children's books, non-fiction works and librettos. He is most famous for his books *A Suitable Boy* and *The Golden Gate*. He has won several awards, notably the Padma Shri and the Sahitya Akademi Award. In addition to being a polyglot, he is also an accomplished musician.

22. Zai Whitaker

Zai Whitaker is a naturalist, educator and writer, perhaps best known for *Kali and the Rat Snake*. She is the co-founder of the Snake Park and the Crocodile Bank in Chennai. She has also written a biography of her husband, naturalist Romulus Whitaker, titled *Snakeman*. This noted conservationist is also involved in promoting education.

Copyright Acknowledgements

This material (Pages 12–22) from *Wings of Fire: An Autobiography* by Dr A.P.J. Abdul Kalam with Arun Tiwari, copyright © Universities Press (India) Private Limited, 1999, is published by arrangement with Universities Press (India) Private Limited.

The original English text of Bhagat Singh's Statement before the Lahore High Court Bench is not traceable. This is retranslated from Hindi by Deepa Agarwal.

Extract 'An Undelivered Speech, 1936' from *Annihilation of Caste: The Annotated Critical Edition* by B.R. Ambedkar: Navayana Publishing Pvt Ltd, 2015, copyright © Navayana Publishing Pvt Ltd, 2014. Reproduced by permission of Navayana Publishing Pvt Ltd, India.

Extract from *Remembering Our Leaders*: Children's Book Trust (CBT), 1996. 'C.V. Raman' by Dilip Salwi from *Remembering Our Leaders* series was first published by CBT and is reproduced by their permission.

Excerpt from *Letters from a Father to His Daughter* by Jawaharlal Nehru: Penguin Books India, 2004, copyright © Priyanka Gandhi Vadra. Reproduced by permission of the copyright holder.

Extract 'Indian Astronomy: Colonial Collaborations' from *The Scientific Edge* by Jayant V. Narlikar: Penguin Books India Pvt Ltd 2003, copyright © Jayant V. Narlikar, 2003. Reproduced by permission of Penguin Books India Pvt Ltd.

Extract 'Memories of Father and a Home' from *On Balance* by Leila Seth: Penguin Books India Pvt Ltd, 2003, copyright © Leila Seth, 2003, 2010. Reproduced by permission of Penguin Books India Pvt Ltd.

Extract 'S Is for Schools' from *Imagining India: Ideas for the New Century* by Nandan Nilekani: Penguin Books India Pvt Ltd, 2009, copyright © Nandan Nilekani, 2008. Reproduced by permission of Penguin Books India Pvt Ltd.

Extract 'Life at My Own Pace' from *The Best of Ruskin Bond* by Ruskin Bond: Penguin Books India Pvt Ltd, 1994, copyright © Ruskin Bond 1994. Reproduced by permission of Penguin Books India Pvt Ltd.

Extract 'Playing for the Flowers' from *Raga'n Josh* by Sheila Dhar: Permanent Black, 2005, copyright © P.N. Dhar 2005. Reproduced by permission of Permanent Black.

Extract 'Kamya Goes Solar' from *MBA at 16* by Subroto Bagchi: Penguin Books India Pvt Ltd, 2012, copyright © Subroto Bagchi, 2012. Reproduced by permission of Penguin Books India Pvt Ltd.

Extract 'Appro J.R.D.' from *How I Taught my Grandmother to Read and Other Stories* by Sudha Murty: Penguin Books India Pvt Ltd, 2004, copyright © Sudha Murty, 2004. Reproduced by permission of Sudha Murty.

Extract 'In the Courts of Emperors' from *Exotic Aliens: The Lion and the Cheetah in India* by Valmik Thapar: Aleph Book Company, 2013, copyright © Valmik Thapar, 2013. Reproduced by permission of Aleph Book Company.

Extract 'Lhasa' from *From Heaven Lake: Travels through Sinkiang and Tibet* by Vikram Seth: copyright © Vikram Seth 1983. Reproduced by permission of Vikram Seth.

Extract "Leave your Tail and Run!' from *Cobra in my Kitchen* by Zai Whitaker: Rupa Publications India Pvt Ltd, 2005, copyright © Zai Whitaker, 2005. Reproduced by permission of Rupa Books India.